Holy Wells

Brendan O'Malley is a retired University Tutor and Dean of Chapel.

He is of Irish descent, Scottish birth and education, and lives in Wales. His interests lie particularly in Celtic spirituality and mystical theology.

In his younger years he was a Cistercian monk and later a Canon of St David's Cathedral. He has a Masters degree in Celtic Christianity and his thesis for Master of Philosophy is on the Holy Wells of Pembrokeshire and the cult of the native saints.

His previous publications include the award-winning *The Animals of St Gregory* (Paulinus Press, 1981); *A Pilgrim's Manual: St David's* (Paulinus Press, 1985); *A Welsh Pilgrim's Manual* (Gomer Press, 1989); *God at Every Gate* (Canterbury Press, 1997); *Pilgrim Guide: St David's* (Canterbury Press, 1997); *Celtic Blessings* (Canterbury Press, 1998); *A Celtic Eucharist* (Canterbury Press, 2001); *A Celtic Primer* (Canterbury Press, 2002) and *Lord of Creation* (Canterbury Press, 2005).

Erratum

Please note that the gazetteer does **NOT** contain information on holy wells in Ireland.

We apologise for this omission.

Holy Wells

A pilgrim's prayer companion and guide

Brendan O'Malley

CANTERBURY
PRESS
Norwich

© in this compilation and script, Brendan O'Malley 2014

This edition published in 2014 by the Canterbury Press Norwich

Editorial office
3rd Floor, Invicta House,
108–114 Golden Lane,
London EC1Y 0TG.

Canterbury Press is an imprint of Hymns Ancient & Modern Ltd
(a registered charity)
13A Hellesdon Park Road, Norwich,
Norfolk, NR6 5DR, UK

www.canterburypress.co.uk

Scripture quotations are from the New Revised Standard Version of
the Bible, copyright 1989 by the Division of Christian Education of
the National Council of the Churches of Christ in the USA. Used by
permission. All rights reserved.

The Psalms are taken from the Standard Book of Common Prayer of
the Episcopal Church of the USA, on which no copyright is claimed.

Brendan O'Malley asserts his right under the Copyright, Designs and
Patents Act, 1998, to be identified as the Author of this work.

British Library Cataloguing in Publication data

A catalogue record for this book is available
from the British Library

978 1 84825 633 0

Printed and bound in Great Britain by
Ashford Colour Press, Gosport

Contents

Contents

To the memory of
my late mother,
Moira Gillespie O'Malley

Foreword

This book is a response to requests made by many people for a small manual of prayer to use when visiting holy wells.

The desire to pray at a holy place is a response to the numinous quality of the place itself and to the presence or aura of holiness inculcated by the holy person who dwelt nearby.

The holy well is a sacramental located in the cathedral of creation; its water often drawn for the healing of failing eyesight, or maladies such as rheumatism or arthritis. It was also used as a sacramental when blessed for baptism or 'holy sprinkling' (i.e. the blessing by holy water as a reminder and renewal of one's baptism). Flowers and ribbons are often affixed to a holy well on festive occasions and wells were frequently used as boundary markers or stations on pilgrimage.

There are many books and gazetteers already published, as well as guides and histories of holy wells; a bibliography of recommended books on holy wells is included, as well as a gazetteer of suitable wells to visit.

The emphasis of this little book is that of creation-centred spirituality; eco-theology or prayer in a sacred landscape. It is not so much a guide as a prompt for the inspiration of contemplative prayer.

My deepest thanks go to my wife Rosemary for drafting the typescript.

List of Illustrations

The publisher and author acknowledge with thanks permission to use photographs. Wikimedia Commons images are available under a Creative Commons Attribution-ShareAlike 3.0 licence.

HOLY WELLS

What mystery pervades a well!
That water lives so far –
A neighbour from another world
Residing in a jar.

Whose limit none have ever seen,
But just his lid of glass –
Like looking every time you please
In an abyss's face!

The grass does not appear afraid,
I often wonder he
Can stand so close and look so bold
At what is awe to me.

Related somehow they may be,
The sedge stands next the sea –
Where he is floorless
And does no timidity betray.

But nature is a stranger yet;
The ones that cite her most
Have never passed her haunted house,
Nor simplified her ghost.

To pity those that know her not
Is helped by the regret
That those who know her, know her less
The nearer her they get.
Emily Dickinson

Introduction

Hasten to the springs, draw from the wells
In God is the wellspring of life,
A spring that can never fail.
Augustine, Commentary on Psalm 42

There were many holy wells in medieval Christendom, a reminder that water is a symbol of grace – a gift of god, springing forth from our mother, the Earth.

Christian tradition has generally avoided the veneration of the various phenomena of nature, and yet springs such as those at Chartres and Lourdes have come to be regarded as sacred because of their connection with miraculous events; and they are still visited by thousands of pilgrims every year.

Water is a symbol of life, a symbol of the soul. Water is essential for human existence. It is therefore not surprising that springs or wells played a central part in the development of society, particularly in the Celtic countries, from the very beginning. Wells and springs were a focal point of Celtic cult practice and ritual. The ancient Celts sited their gods in streams, springs and wells, and there is an interweaving of Christian and pagan belief in many holy well ritual practices.

I prayed for a plot of land, not so very large, containing a
garden; and near the household a spring of fresh water,
and a bit of woodland to complete it.
Horace (65 BC)

1

HOLY WELLS

The Celtic saints were imbued with the mysterious reality of the continuing presence of God: His imminent presence in the world and therefore with the incarnational nature of all creation. In the way they recognized this mystery their world view was closer to our own than that of many in the intervening centuries with their more intellectual and doctrinal formulations. They had a deep and abiding love of Holy Writ, evidenced in the beautifully illuminated texts of the period, and they cultivated the love of learning and of piety. But more important to a rural people very close to nature, very down to earth and dwelling in a sacral environment, every well-spring, wood and stone took on a mystical significance. No doubt this proceeded from their pagan past but that was transformed; its numinous properties spiritualized by Christian prayer. The Scottish Gaelic language has a phrase 'Are you going to church?' which when literally translated says 'Are you going to the stones?' The awareness of the whole world as Incarnational was linked in to a tremendous 'spirit of place'. Holy wells locate for us this long and deep spiritual and cultural tradition.

Many country churches and chapels had a holy well, many taken over from the Druids and Christianized. The waters were used for baptism, holy blessing by sprinkling, for the healing of rheumatism and eye maladies as well as the needs of general use. Water naturally alleviates many ailments. Early man must have been a very different figure from today's sanitized creature: unwashed, easily infected if he cut himself. As he domesticated animals instead of merely hunting them their diseases were also a concern for him. A good wash makes one feel better; pure clean water is essential to life. Spring water contains such minerals as calcium, iron, magnesium, iodine and chromium, which are beneficial to the human body in the correct amounts. Health-giving springs would have been much frequented and cherished. Many centuries later, such curative waters would become the focus of spa towns such as Bath and Leamington Spa in England, Llandrindod, Llanwrtyd or Builth Wells in Wales, and in many other places where visitors could benefit from the trace elements in the water.

A walker will surely sooner or later pass by a holy well. The dedication of the well may be obscure but the well important enough to be remembered. It may have its saint's name attached to it. The generation that remember the daily uses of the well invariably comment on the purity and the goodness of the water, although the healing traditions may be forgotten. At some wells the water was once renowned for healing the sick, both man and beast. Examples of such wells are to be found particularly in the 'Celtic fringe' of Wales, Scotland and Cornwall. Ireland has them in abundance.

A natural history of holy wells also exists. Many amphibians, which must keep their skin moist or perish, live in or near springs and wells. These creatures, like the fish and eels traditionally associated with certain sacred wells, inevitably enter local legend. A man who coughed up a frog after imbibing the water of St Justinian's well on Ramsey Island, Pembrokeshire, was said to have received an instant cure. On travelling around the country researching the wells, newts, toads, frogs, lizards and even a tortoise (at St Salmon's well) were encountered; their presence apparently testifying to the purity of the spring water.

3

HOLY WELLS

After Christianity came to Britain, the veneration of many ancient wells probably remained strong. A well that had been the focus of pagan cultic practice for healing, cursing or prophecy may have become 'blessed' by association with Christianity. The survival of the well cult is partly due to the cult of the saint who was possibly one of the peregrini who wandered over the landscape, often alone and sometimes with a group of disciples. At selected places, close by a stream or font, they would set up a beehive cell and possibly a wooden preaching cross. The spot where the holy one had dwelt became sanctified by use, and in time a chapel would replace the site of the cell, first in wattle and daub, then in oak and if the place grew attractive, ultimately a stone building would appear. The church generally retained the dedication name of its original founder. Sometimes the patron saint's name would be changed after several years to that of a major saint (e.g. The Blessed Virgin Mary) but the name of the adjacent holy well would retain the name of the original Celtic or Anglo-Saxon saint.

The survival of the well cult is partly due to the cult of the saint who may have used the well for their everyday purposes, as well as sanctifying it through their use of it for the Sacrament of Baptism. It also became customary to carry water from the holy well to the church for this purpose, and this has continued in certain areas until recent times.

During the Middle Ages and later, wells appeared in the visible life of the people; they were a 'touchstone' of the supernatural and, largely due to their actual or supposed healing properties, became the doctors of the peasantry. The well cult had an undisputed effect on the human mind and the tales and suppositions relating to the wells deeply influenced the ways and thoughts of our ancestors. They were indeed the stuff of legend. After all a legend has of necessity an historical or topographical connection. It refers imaginary events to a real person, associates fanciful stories with an existing place.

The 'Lives of the Saints' were generally written to popularize the cult of certain saints, and so churches and wells that bore their names may have owed association more to the hagiographers than to the saints themselves. The tradition of the saint's name connected with churches and wells may have sprung more from a clerical writer than from the saint actually having ever lived at the place bearing his or her dedication. We simply do not know whether the dedications of many wells owe more to the 'Lives of the Saints' than to the 'Age of the Saints'. We do not know whether a holy well bearing a saint's name was ever used by the person for whom it was named. The importance of the holy well and its dedication to a particular saint was not so much concerned with what the saint *did* there or what biographical history would record, as with the *ideal* he or she represented. The holy wells may have been symbols of divine power working through the action of the saints, but hagiographers did not hesitate to add on the word 'miracle' to what they considered to be marvellous occurrences if they wished to communicate their confidence in the saint.

Christ is everywhere present, but he is particularly close in places where prayer has been practised regularly, and his presence is also keenly felt in the daily round of human tasks and at the important occasions for recognizing the presence of God, such as when the psalms are recited. At the very centre of Celtic spirituality there is this intense sense of presence. The peregrini hermit or holy person was God intoxicated; their life embraced on all sides by the divine Being. Everything they did was executed in God's presence not only when they got up and went to sleep, but when communing with nature and practising the common round of gardening or cooking their meal. They realized the presence of God both outwardly and inwardly; their identity was in their relationship with God.

The Liturgy is a cosmic event.
Cardinal Kurt Koch

Sometimes, by a holy well,
I experience the mystery of the presence
Of God, and listen to the sound
Of Creation's vibrant spell.

In the silence of my heart mystical
Truth changes and transforms
Into a stream of living water
Springing up from the well of Love Eternal.

Itinerary

The Blessing of those beginning a journey

BENEDICTUS

Blessed by the Lord the God of Israel: for he has come to his people to set them free.
He has raised up for us a mighty Saviour: born of the house of his servant David.
Through his holy prophets he promised of old that he would save us from our enemies: from the hands of all that hate us.
He promised to show mercy to our forebears: and to remember his holy covenant.
This was the oath he swore to our father Abraham: to set us free from the hands of our enemies,
Free to worship him without fear: holy and righteous in his sight all the days of our life.
You my child shall be called the prophet of the most high: for you will go before the Lord to prepare his way,
To give his people knowledge of salvation: by the forgiveness of all their sins.
In the tender compassion of our God: the dawn from on high shall break upon us,
To shine on those who dwell in darkness and the shadow of death: and to guide our feet into the way of peace.

HOLY WELLS

ANTIPHON

May the almighty and merciful God direct us in the way of peace and happiness, and may the Angel Raphael accompany us on the way so that we may return home again with peace, and health, and joy.

President	Lord, have mercy on us.
All	**Christ, have mercy on us.**
President	Lord, have mercy on us.
All	**Our Father ....**
President	Save your servants
All	**Who hope in you, O Lord.**
President	Send us help from your holy place, O Lord.
All	**And out of Sion protect us.**
President	Be for us, O Lord, a tower of strength
All	**From the face of the enemy.**
President	Let not the enemy prevail against us.
All	**Nor the son of iniquity have power to hurt us.**
President	Blessed be the Lord God day by day.
All	**May the God of our salvation bless our journey.**
President	Show us your ways, O God.
All	**And teach us your paths.**
President	May our ways be directed
All	**Into keeping your judgements.**

ITINERARY

President	May the crooked paths be made straight.
All	**And the rough ways be made smooth.**
President	He has given the Angels charge over you
All	**To keep you in all your ways.**
President	Lord, hear my prayer.
All	**And let my cry come unto you.**
President	The Lord be with you.
All	**And also with you.**
	Let us pray.

COLLECT

We beseech you, O Lord, give ear to our prayers; direct the travel of your servants in the sure way of salvation; that in the midst of all the diversities of journey and of this life we may always be protected by your help.

We beseech you, Almighty God, grant that your servants may walk in the way of salvation, and that, following the exhortations of your precursor, St John the Baptist, may securely reach Him whom St John the Baptist foretold, our Lord Jesus Christ your Son.

BLESSING

Heavenly Father, you have shown your love for us by giving us Jesus to be our way to you. Guide us as we begin this journey. Bless us with peace and joy as we travel, and bring us home safely. We ask this grace through Jesus, our brother and our Lord.

Bless us in the Name of the Father, the Son and the Holy

HOLY WELLS

Spirit, the One and the Three. May God give us to drink of his cup, may the sun shine bright upon us, may the night call down peace. And when we come to his household, may the door be open wide for us to go into our joy.

President	Let us proceed in peace.
All	**In the Name of Christ. Amen.**

King of the Elements

O God of the elements
O God of the mysteries
O God of the well-springs
O King of Kings
Thy joy the joy
Thy light the light
Thy war the war
Thy peace the peace
Thy pain the pain
Thy love the love
That lasts for ever
To the end of ends.

ITINERARY

Transcendent Earth

The gurgling stream beneath the tree
Down-fallen across the well in the glen,
Plays haunting music wild and free
Drugging the heart with its throbbing refrain.

This sad silent music pulsating yet still;
Moves through the grass in swirl and eddy,
Sings in the babbling of the rill,
And echoes high-curling enchantedly.

Then moving, mysterious, descending deep
Down through the blood by pulsing veins
In a rhythmic, languid, snake-like creep
Out onto the earth its liquid drains.

To dwell in the kingdom beneath the feet
Seducing souls commune
With the living earth, the life of the seed,
The fragrant flowers in bloom.

Then floating majestically upward-sublime
It merges in cloud of soft pink hue,
Heavenward groping in spiralling climb
To vanish – still singing, in pastel blue.

Brendanus Scotus

Well Customs

*What sublime truths and wholesome themes
lodge in thy mystical deep streams.*
Henry Vaughan

The traditional manner of worship at the holy wells and pilgrimage sites in Celtic countries is to follow, one after the other in single file, being careful to keep the well on the right hand side, following the course of the sun. This is an ancient ritual. The pilgrim may repeat short repetitive prayers such as the Jesus Prayer (Lord Jesus Christ, Son of God, have mercy on me a sinner); or the Hail Mary; or the Our Father; or the Glory Be; or Kyrie Eleison, Christe Eleison, Kyrie Eleison.

Some of the well water may then be drunk (if considered pure enough!) or the dipping of the hand in the water and using it for blessing oneself or sprinkling on the forehead.

Often there is a special tree or bush near the well on which may be hung a votive offering. Handkerchiefs or beads and the like are often found at holy wells as if this were the most natural thing to do. In some cases there is a carved stone at which a pilgrim may pray or round which they may walk. Sometimes a cairn is found and a stone added to the heap by pilgrims. It is known that stones and trees may be honoured because of their associations with the well's saint.

WELL CUSTOMS

Celtic Idyll

I wish, O Son of the living God, O ancient eternal King,
For a hidden little hut in the wilderness
That it may be my dwelling.
An all-grey little lark to be by its side,
A clear pool to wash away sins through
The grace of the Holy Spirit.

From a seventh-century Irish poem

Arrival at a Holy Well

'Take off your sandals, because you are standing on holy ground.'
Exodus 3.5

READING

O God of unchangeable power and eternal light, look favourably on thy whole creation, that wonderful and sacred mystery, and by the continual operation of thy perpetual providence carry out the work of our true healing, and let the whole world feel and see that things which were cast down are being raised up, and things which had grown old are being made new, and all things are returning to perfection through Christ from whom they took their origin, to whom be all honour and glory.   Amen.

PSALM

Come, let us sing to the Lord,
Let us shout for joy to the rock of our salvation.
Let us come before his presence with thanksgiving
And raise a loud shout to him with psalms.
For the Lord is a great God,
And a great king above all gods.

HOLY WELLS

In his hand are the caverns of the earth,
And the heights of the hills are his also.
The sea is his, for he made it,
And his hands have moulded the dry land.
Come, let us bow down, and bend the knee,
And kneel before the Lord our Maker.
For he is our God,
And we are the people of his pasture and the sheep of his hand.
O, that today you would hearken to his voice!
Psalm 95.1–7

READING

But now thus says the Lord,
He who created you, O Jacob,
He who formed you, O Israel:
Do not fear, for I have redeemed you:
I have called you by name, you are mine,
When you pass through the waters, I will be with you;
And through the rivers, they shall not overwhelm you;
When you walk through fire you shall not be burned,
And the flame shall not consume you.
For I am the Lord your God,
The Holy One of Israel, your Saviour.
I give Egypt as your ransom,
Ethiopia and Seba in exchange for you.
Because you are precious in my sight,
And honoured, and I love you,
I give people in return for you,
Nations in exchange for your life.

ARRIVAL AT A HOLY WELL

Do not fear, for I am with you;
I will bring your offspring from the east,
And from the west I will gather you;
I will say to the north, 'Give them up',
And to the south, 'Do not withhold;
Bring my sons from far away
And my daughters from the end of the earth –
Everyone who is called by my name,
Whom I created for my glory, whom I formed and made.'
Isaiah 43.1–7 (the pilgrimage back from Babylon)

| President | We give thanks to you, heavenly Father, for all your blessings on this journey. |
| *All* | **We give thanks.** |

| President | For the enjoyment we have had together. |
| *All* | **We give thanks.** |

| President | For the fellowship we have experienced. |
| *All* | **We give thanks.** |

| President | For the greater sense of our unity in Christ that we have developed. |
| *All* | **We give thanks.** |

| President | For our deeper appreciation of the presence of the Cosmic Christ at the centre of matter. |
| *All* | **We give thanks.** |

HOLY WELLS

NUNC DIMITTIS

Lord, now lettest thou thy servant depart in peace: according to thy word.

For mine eyes have seen thy salvation;

Which thou has prepared before the face of all peoples.

To be a light to lighten the Gentiles; and to be the glory of thy people Israel.

Glory be to the Father, and to the Son, and to the Holy Spirit;

As it was in the beginning, is now and ever shall be;

World without end.   Amen.

A Celtic Blessing

May the road rise up to meet you
May the wind be always at your back
May the sun shine warm upon your face
And the rain fall soft upon your fields
And until we meet again
May God hold you in the palm of his hand.
Amen.

Well Blessing

Bless the Lord you springs,
Sing praise to him and highly exalt him for ever.
Prayer of Azariah 56

Celtic spirituality is deeply influenced by the sacramental nature of the landscape and although the average person may be largely unconscious of the effect of symbols and signs, nevertheless they are often deeply affected by the hidden or mystical influence of the energy of Creation.

The well spring is a symbol of the basic source of life. The site of the *peregrini* or Celtic saints' dwelling is often marked by a holy well to which the saint was divinely led and from which they derived natural refreshment. Water is necessary for physical survival, let alone cleanliness, health and comfort. It is also necessary for baptism. The sacramental intermingling of the natural and the supernatural is very much in the Celtic Christian tradition. Water is not brought from somewhere and poured in a font; it is living water, springing forth from the ground. One may go down steps to the well. For as may be found in many ancient baptisteries, baptism is both a cleansing and a going down into the death of Christ and a rising with him in new life. Holy sprinkling is a natural sacramental action when, by the use of water as a sign and pledge of God's grace, we are enabled to receive inward and spiritual healing.

Symbolic purification by washing with water taken from the well may take place. This act is part of an ancient process from time past when Christianity was displacing paganism and the holy well became a sign of the victory of the saint who blessed the well and used the water to baptize new Christians.

Water may be blessed and used as a reminder of our baptism when God made us his children and brothers and sisters of Jesus Christ. It is through baptism that we share in the work of Christ, praise God and become one with the whole of Creation both mystically (i.e. inwardly) and physically (i.e. outwardly).

Holy Sprinkling

PRAYER

Graciously hear us, Lord, God of all Creation, that as we rejoice in the memory of blessed (*N*) we may be enlightened in spiritual understanding and devotion. Through Christ our Lord.
In the Name of the Father, and of the Son, and of the Holy Spirit.

President	The Lord be with you.
All	**And also with you.**

READING

With joy you will draw water from the wells of salvation. And you will say on that day: give thanks to the Lord, call on his name; make known his deeds among the nations; proclaim that his name is exalted.

Isaiah 12.3

GOSPEL

Come to me, all you that are weary and are carrying heavy burdens and I will give you rest. Take my yoke upon you, and learn from me; for I am gentle and humble in heart, and you will find rest for your souls. For my yoke is easy, and my burden is light.

Matthew 11.28

DEDICATION

Blessed are you, Lord our God, Creator of heaven and earth, through your goodness you have given us this well for our right use and the glorification of your Name as King of the Elements.

We dedicate this well in your Name and in the name of ... (*local saint*) as a place of peace and a symbol of purity, refreshment, blessing and joy for all.

To prepare ourselves for this holy sprinkling let us call to mind our sins ... (*pause*).

President	Lord Jesus, you healed the sick. Lord, have mercy.
All	**Lord, have mercy.**
President	Lord Jesus, you forgave sinners. Christ, have mercy.
All	**Christ, have mercy.**

HOLY WELLS

President	Lord Jesus, you gave us yourself to heal and bring us to strength.
	Lord, have mercy.
All	**Lord, have mercy.**

May almighty God have mercy on us, forgive us our sins, and bring us to everlasting life.   Amen.

Blessed are you, Lord, God of all Creation, through the waters of our baptism you have raised us to new life in Christ Jesus. Let this holy sprinkling remind us of your love shown to us when we were baptized. Help us, Father, to live according to your way which is the truth and the life according to our Lord, and Saviour Jesus Christ.

BLESSING

Father, bless + this well and let it be a place of prayer and peace. May it be a focus for stillness and reflection. Open our hearts to your Spirit, and lead us on the paths of Christ your Son.
All praise and glory be yours for ever.   Amen.

(*The assembled pilgrims are sprinkled with the blessed water to the words*):

May Almighty God at the intercession of .... (saint's name associated with the well) grant you health and peace.

WELL BLESSING

Or: (a sign of the cross with water may be made on the forehead)

A small drop of water
To thy forehead, beloved,
Meet for the Father, Son and Spirit,
The Triune of power.
A small drop of water,
To encompass my beloved,
Meet for the Father, Son and Spirit.
The Triune of power.
A small drop of water
To fill thee with each grace,
Meet for the Father, Son and Spirit.
The Triune of power.

Carmina Gadelica.III. 22

Lord, in your mercy give us living water, always springing up as a fountain of healing; free us body, mind and spirit, from every danger and admit us to your presence in purity of heart.
Grant this through Christ our Lord.   Amen.

There is no well, no pool
No water that fulfils my thirst
But Thee, dear Lord of all Creation.   Amen.

HOLY WELLS

On a Fallen Tree

Once, long ago, the rain poured down a storm shattered sky
Mingling with sap bled from a murdered spruce
Tumbled by lightning and felled from on high,
Feeding the soil with its life-giving juice.
But now; low crouched in a deep sylvan glade reflecting
Flakes of sunlight seeping through the trees
It lives again, aglow a mossy green in the spell-casting
Shade, with bracken veiling its prayer-bent knees.
Brendanus Scotus

Prayer Stones

The subatomic particles we see in nature, the quartz, the electrons are nothing but musical notes on a tiny vibrating string.
Michio Kaku

God is sounding throughout the universe. 'In the beginning was the Word and the Word was God.' Word is the explanation of God and is always giving birth to itself. Earth is but the frozen echo of the silent voice of God. The life Absolute, the Supreme Being, the I AM, from which has sprung all that is felt, seen and perceived and into which all again merges in time, is a silent, motionless and eternal life. Every motion that springs from this silent life is a vibration and a creator of vibrations.

The mineral, vegetable, animal and human kingdoms are the gradual changes of vibrations, and the vibrations of each change differ from one another in their weight, breadth, length, colour, effect, sound and rhythm. Human beings are not only formed of vibrations, but live and move in them. They are surrounded by them as fish are surrounded by water, and humanity contains them as the tank contains water.

All things being derived from and formed of vibrations have sound hidden within them, as fire is hidden in flint, and each atom of the universe confesses by its tone: 'My sole origin is sound.' If any solid or hollow sonorous body is struck it will answer back: 'I am sound.'

Sound has its birth, death, sex, form, planet, colour, child-hood, youth and age; but that volume of sound which is in the abstract sphere beyond the sphere of the concrete is the origin and basis of all sound. When visiting a holy well or walking in the woods, listen to the sound of the birds singing their hearts out overhead in the trees; to the water gurgling as it flows over stones; to the sea as the waves fall joyfully on the rocks with its repetitive sonorous message. Listen to the constant murmuring of the wind. Hear the bright Sound of God; the glory of God fully alive and well. It is 'theo-phonic'. The Sound of God is always active, always altering in the sound, never dead or inert and always in the present.

To stand or sit and listen to the sound of the wind and rustling grasses and leaves, or the soughing over stones, is to experience theophony, the supreme symbol of the Holy Spirit. To breathe in and out, conscious that you are breathing in and out the presence of God is true prayer which is the respiration of the soul.

> *God is Breath,*
> *For the breath of the wind is shared by all,*
> *Goes everywhere, nothing shuts it in,*
> *Nothing holds it prisoner.*
> Maximus the Confessor

This breath is not just the air that fills the lungs giving energy to the body. It is the breath of the universe. Once this sound is heard, it brands the listener with a name on a white stone, which is the secret pin number that releases true identity. 'Let anyone who has an ear listen to what the Spirit is saying … to everyone who conquers I will give … a white stone, and on the white stone is written a new name that no one knows except the one who receives it' (Revelation 2.17).

The sound of the wind and the white stone suggest a theophony, a theology of nature as *sound*: similar to a 'theophany'. 'Every visible and invisible creature can be called a theophany' (John Scotus Eriugena). A theophany is a showing of divine presence. The uncreated light that holds all creation in being may awaken our awareness at any time of place. 'With you is the well of life, and in your light we see light' (Psalm 36.9).

All created being is a vehicle of uncreated energy, the grace of God. His love shines through all creation. This eternal uncreated light is at the centre of every particle, proton, every electron, each not-yet-named subatomic particle.

> *Now the eternal light manifests itself to the world in two ways, through the Scriptures and creatures. For the divine knowledge cannot be restored in us except by the letters of scripture and the sight of creatures. Learn the words of scripture and understand their meaning in your soul, there you will discover the Word. Know the forms and beauty of sensible things by your physical senses, and see there the Word of God. And in all these things Truth itself proclaims things, and apart from whom there is nothing for you to contemplate since he is himself all things. He himself is the being of all things.*
>
> John Scotus Eriugena (Homily to the prologue to the Gospel of John)

It is therefore natural for the pilgrim to the holy well to pick up a small quartz stone or pebble and hold it in the palm of the hand as a constant reminder and channel of the uncreated energy of God found in that place.

The Creator is the primal music that co-relates in every vibration/sound and in the name of every living thing. It is the sound of the Divine Name, the I AM vibrating throughout the cosmos. There was a saying that circulated among the early Christians, attributed to Christ though not found in the Gospels: 'Lift the stone and you will find me, cut the wood and there am I.'

Among the pre-Christian dwellers of this land perhaps it was believed that a God or Gods was actually present in the wells, in the stone. We Christians cannot believe in a multiplicity of Gods but we still believe in the same imminent presence. Well springs are holy places not just by virtue of the fact that a holy saint lived and prayed there; but by virtue of the fact of what they are, living waters springing up from the earth and the gift of God. That is what makes for a holy place.

It is perhaps a good thing to remember that in the Greek Fathers, and perhaps in the Latin Fathers too, everywhere and every fountain has its own particular guardian angel who is the symbol of the living embodiment of God's Presence in that place. We find God in everything. Mysticism is not merely visions and ecstasy; the mystical approach is to find the extraordinary in the ordinary. To find eternity in the familiar objects we handle and use every day.

In many Celtic churches small white pebbles may be found. These white stones are placed there as offerings by pilgrims, having been carried as prayer stones to the holy place. They 'signify the eternal substance of existence, at a level deeper than ego-consciousness'. They are a means of communication with this eternal substance and a link between Creator and bearer. White pebbles of quartz may be used as an aid to concentrated contemplation. Quartz is compressed sound and is a vehicle of the I AM, the Alpha and the Omega, the beginning and the end of all created being; the Sound of God.

How can a prayer stone help our prayer?

There are many aids to help the practice of contemplative prayer and all of them, whether they be an icon, prayer beads or stones, are there to help us to focus and concentrate (concentre) at the level of the heart. This enables our minds and bodies to become centred, still, relaxed and attentive to the One Thing Necessary.

A pebble or small piece of quartz can be an aid to centring prayer.

Allow the stone to rest lightly in the hand and be aware of the thousands of years it has taken to compress this vibration of sound into stone. Remember that the whole of creation is vibrating at many levels of sound. The mineral, vegetable, animal and all physical and human kingdoms are the gradual changes of vibrations. We live and move and have our being in them. All matter, all being, have sound hidden within them; as fire is hidden in flint and each atom of the universe confesses in its tone: 'My origin is sound.'

We encounter the Creator through sound.

A Sacrament is the promise of an encounter with the Divine in the Now. A prayer stone may become a sacramental through the sacred intention of its use. Stones are mentioned in the Bible:

> 'Come to him that living stone …'
> 'Become yourself a living stone …'
> 'Christ the corner stone …'
> 'The white stone in which your new name lies hidden.'

PRAYER STONES

I am in the stone
I am in the wood
I am in the sun
I am in the dancing
I am in all things –
This is my freedom
This is my strength
This my journey
This my discovery
This myself.
Taken from Taliesin's Creed

Creation prays with us and we pray with Creation.
Pope Benedict XVI

Blessing of a Prayer Stone

1   Cleanse with water (preferably Holy Water).
2   Dedicate the stone to its future use.
3   Blessing.

Father in heaven, we praise you for sending your Spirit into our hearts, may your Word teach us to pray.

Bless + this stone and teach us to use it as an aid to sincere and devoted prayer. May we continue to grow in prayer and be pleasing to you in our lives.

All praise and glory are yours, Father, through Christ our Saviour, in the Holy Spirit. God for ever and ever.   Amen.

Or:

Let us pray to our Lord God, Father in heaven, who has given this/these stones as an aid to prayer.

(*All pause for a moment in silent prayer*)

Blessed are you, Lord God, King of the elements. You have made all things for your glory.

Bless + this/these stones and grant that we may use it/them for your service and for the good of all creation.

Lord God, we praise you through Christ our Lord.   Amen.

PRAYER STONES

When carrying a prayer stone a Christian mantra or short repetitive prayer may be repeated inwardly. For example, The Jesus Prayer: 'Lord Jesus Christ, Son of God, have mercy on me a sinner', or 'Maranatha' (Come, Lord, Come).

Or:

'I Am that I Am' (the Name God gave himself when he appeared to Moses at the burning bush).

The main thing with a prayer practice is our state of mind or intention, and the openness of our heart to God. The more open to God – the more we will receive.

The use of God's created objects can be of some help in disposing ourselves – for they possess a created energy by the hand of God, a vibration still present from the beginning of Creation. If it helps us focus an inner state of prayer then all help from created matter should be gracefully received.

> *Like living stones, let yourselves be built into a spiritual house.*
> 1 Peter 2.1

Prayers for Healing

Open now the crystal fountain, whence the healing stream
doth flow.
William Williams Pantycelyn

As a deer longs for the running brooks: so longs my
soul for you, O God.
My soul is thirsty for God: when shall I come and see
his face?
My tears have been my food day and night: while they
ask me all day long 'Where now is your God?'
Why are you so full of heaviness my soul: and why so
unquiet within me?
O put your trust in God: for I will praise him yet, who is
my deliverer and my God.
Deep calls to deep in the roar of your waters: all your
waves and breakers have gone over me.
From Psalm 42

HOLY WELLS

LAYING ON OF HANDS

I am Light of the cosmos,
Who dances
Flickering down through the head,
Breathed,
Flowing in
Myriad colours to the heart
Healing
The world
Through the laying on of hands.

(Hands may be laid gently on the head of the supplicant or held lightly over the head with the following words)

Through the laying on of hands and through our prayer receive the gift of the healing Spirit of God.

May the Holy Spirit the giver of life and healing fill you with light and love and make you whole.

Or:

May the Holy Spirit be a wellspring of healing within you taking away anything that is harming or disturbing you. We ask this in the Name of Jesus Christ our Lord.

May the healing stream of the Holy Spirit flow through your body, mind and spirit, making you whole. In the Name of our Lord, Jesus Christ.   Amen.

PRAYERS FOR HEALING

READING

The Spirit glides over the water.
Immersion is the return to the formless; the dissolution of form;
The plunging into night;
The birth of the new bud; therefore also creative.
Depth is more Godlike than height;
Sinking is more holy than climbing.
The Creator God, a great underground river
Awaits our sinking more than our climbing.
The reason we can trust the sinking is that at the very depths,
At the bottom, my ground and God's are the same.
We need to return to our origins,
The darkness of the womb.
Deep contentment: then healing.

LET US PRAY

Lord, in your mercy give us living water, always springing up as a fountain of salvation. Free us, body and soul, from every danger and admit us to your presence in purity of heart. Grant this through Christ our Lord.   Amen.

CONTEMPLATION

From tradition we know that Celtic saints prayed in rivers, by waterfalls and by holy wells. This practice may well have been a continuation taken from the Druid's veneration of sacred waters.

HOLY WELLS

The explanation of God
Is the Word. The Sound
That loved the Universe into
Being and the sound of this cosmic music
Is the uncreated energy of grace;
The stuff of God emanating
The essence of the supreme Being.

Let that sound resonate
Through you in the stillness
Of Creation that a spiritual
Change may take place.
A Vibrant experience not
An intellectual one where
We understand in the heart.

The well of the heart
Is at the centre of our self
Where we understand not what
Is uttered but feel in
Response to what we silently
Listen to. Nothing can deceive
Us when we sit alone and
Listen. For we are
Servants guided by the King
Of the Elements.
Brendanus Scotus

God in the depths of us receives God who comes to us:
It is God contemplating God.
Blessed John Ruysbroeck

PRAYERS FOR HEALING

The Lord will guide you continually, and satisfy your needs in parched places, and make your bones strong; and you shall be like a watered garden, like a spring of water, whose waters never fail.
Isaiah 58.11

Holy Well Stations

A 'station', as on railways, is just a stopping place; whether one stops for a picnic or for thought. Often we want to sit down and meditate when on pilgrimage. How we use the 'stations' will depend on how many stops or 'stations' are made on the way to a holy well or a holy place, and the formality or informality of its use on the company and circumstance.

A greeting sentence, a psalm, the collect, responses and a versicle 'Let us go forth in peace' may be as well read on its own, as aloud with a group of fellow pilgrims. Prayers for resting on the way are in a further section, as well as a selection of appropriate poetry.

Give me my scallop shell of quiet,
My staff of faith to walk upon,
My scrip of joy, immortal diet, my bottle of salvation,
My gown of glory, hope's true gage,
And thus I'll take my pilgrimage.
Sir Walter Raleigh

Station One

SENTENCE

I am the Alpha and the Omega, the Beginning and the End.
To the thirsty I will give water as a gift from the spring of the
Well of Life.
Revelation 21.6–7

READING

Draw me whether through love or grief, draw me through
bitterness or sweetness, through adversity or prosperity,
through ways narrow or broad, through things easy or hard
… draw me through what and with what you will, so that I
have you only in my life and all my hope here in the future,
that I may never be separated from the fire of your love,
because you are all I desire.
Royal MS, eighth century

PSALM

The Lord is my Shepherd,
I shall not want.
He makes me lie down in green pastures
And leads me beside still waters.
He revives my soul
And guides me along right pathways for his name's sake.
Though I walk through the valley of the shadow of death,
I shall fear no evil,
For you are with me;
Your rod and your staff, they comfort me.

HOLY WELL STATIONS: ONE

You spread a table before me in the presence of those
Who trouble me;
You have anointed my head with oil,
And my cup is running over.
Surely goodness and mercy shall follow me all the days of
my life,
And I will dwell in the house of the Lord for ever.
Psalm 23

PRAYER

We beseech Thee, O Lord, to send Thy grace before us
to guide our steps, and sending it with us, be pleased to
accompany us on our way; that by the protection of Thy
mercy, we may rejoice both in our progress and in our safety.
Through our Lord Jesus Christ. Amen.

President	Direct my steps according to Thy word; and let no iniquity have dominion over me.
All	**I rejoiced at the things that were said to me: we shall go into the house of the Lord, Alleluia.**
President	Let us go forth in peace.
All	**In the Name of Christ. Amen.**

Station Two

SENTENCE

For the lamb at the centre of the throne will be their shepherd
and he will guide them to springs of the water of life.
Revelation 7.17

READING (Rivers of Living Waters)

On the last day of the festival, the great day when Jesus
was standing there, he cried out, 'Let anyone who is thirsty
come to me, and let the one who believes in me drink. As
the scripture has said, "Out of the believer's heart shall flow
rivers of living water."' Now he said this about the Spirit,
which believers in him were to receive, as yet there was no
Spirit, because Jesus had not yet been glorified.
John 7.37–39

PSALM

As the deer long for the water-brooks,
So longs my soul for you, O God.
My soul is athirst for God, athirst for the living God;
When shall I come to appear before the presence of God?
My tears have been my food day and night,
While all day long they say to me,
'Where now is your God?'
I pour out my soul when I think on these things.
How I went with the multitude and led them into the house
of God,
With the voice of praise and thanksgiving,
Among those who keep holy-day.
Why are you so full of heaviness, O my soul?
And why are you so disquieted within me?

HOLY WELL STATIONS: TWO

Put your trust in God,
For I will give thanks to him
Who is the help of my countenance, and my God.
My soul is heavy within me;
Therefore I will remember you from the land of Jordan,
And from the peak of Mizar among the heights of Hermon.
One deep calls to another in the noise of your cataracts;
All your rapids and floods have gone over me.
The Lord grants his loving-kindness in the daytime;
In the night season his song is with me,
A prayer to the God of my life.
I will say to the God of my strength,
'Why have you forgotten me?
And why do I go so heavily while the enemy
Oppresses me?'
While my bones are being broken,
My enemies mock me to my face;
All day long they mock me
And say to me, 'Where now is your God?'
Why are you so full of heaviness, O my soul?
And why are you so disquieted within me?
Put your trust in God,
For I will yet give thanks to him,
Who is the help of my countenance, and my God.
Psalm 42

PRAYER

Lord of light, of wind and waters. Protect us and be with us
as we journey to your heavenly kingdom where you live and
reign. One God, world without end.   Amen.

President	Let us go forth in peace.
All	**In the Name of Christ. Amen.**

Station Three

SENTENCE

Wisdom is the wellspring of life to one who hast it.

Proverbs 16.22

READING

They deliberately ignore this fact, that by the Word of God heavens existed long ago and an earth was formed out of water and by means of water.

2 Peter 3–5

PSALM

O God, my God; eagerly I seek you;
My soul thirsts for you, my flesh faints for you,
As in a barren and dry land where there is no water.
Therefore I have gazed upon you in your holy place,
That I might behold your power and your glory.
For your loving-kindness is better than life itself;
My lips shall give you praise.
So will I bless you as long as I live
And lift up my hands in your name.
My soul is content, as with marrow and fatness,
And my mouth praises you with joyful lips,
When I remember you upon my bed,
And meditate on you in the night watches.
For you have been my helper,
And under the shadow of your wings I will rejoice.
My soul clings to you,
Your right hand holds me fast.

Psalm 63.1–8

Tirechan's Creed

Our God is the God of all humans,
The God of heaven and earth,
The God of sea and rivers,
The God of the sun and moon,
The God of all the heavenly bodies,
The God of the lofty mountains,
The God of the lowly valleys.
God is above the heavens;
And he is beneath the heavens.
Heaven and earth and sea,
And everything that is in them,
Such he has as his above.
He inspires all things,
He gives life to all things,
He stands beneath all things.
He enlightens the light of the sun,
He strengthens the light of the night and the stars,
He makes wells in the arid land and dry islands in the sea,
And he places the stars in the service of the greater lights.
He has a Son who is co-eternal with himself,
And similar in all respects to himself;
And neither is the Son younger than the Father,
Nor is the Father older than the Son;
And the Holy Spirit breathes in them.
And the Father and the Son and Holy Spirit are inseparable.
Amen.

From the Book of Armagh, AD 670

Station Four

SENTENCE

Above all else guard your heart, for it is the wellspring of life.
Proverbs 4.23

READING

Once Jesus was asked by the Pharisees when the Kingdom of God was coming and he answered, 'The Kingdom of God is not coming with things that can be observed; nor will they say, "Look, here it is!" or "There it is!" For, in fact, the Kingdom of God is among you.'
John 17.20–21

PSALM

Ascribe to the Lord, you gods,
Ascribe to the Lord glory and strength.
Ascribe to the Lord the glory due his name;
Worship the Lord in the beauty of holiness.
The voice of the Lord is upon the waters;
The God of glory thunders;
The Lord is upon the mighty waters.
The voice of the Lord is a powerful voice;
The voice of the Lord is a voice of splendour.
The voice of the Lord breaks the cedar trees;
The Lord breaks the cedars of Lebanon;
He makes Lebanon skip like a calf,
And Mount Hermon like a young wild ox.
The voice of the Lord splits the flames of fire;

HOLY WELL STATIONS: FOUR

The voice of the Lord shakes the wilderness;
The Lord shakes the wilderness of Kadesh.
The voice of the Lord makes the oak trees writhe
And strips the forests bare.
And in the temple of the Lord
All are crying, 'Glory!'
The Lord sits enthroned above the flood;
The Lord sits enthroned as king for evermore.
The Lord shall give strength to his people;
The Lord shall give his people the blessing of peace.
Psalm 29

PRAYER

Lord, come to our rescue, and we shall sing psalms all the days of our life in the house of the Lord.
Isaiah 38.20

President	Let us go forth in peace.
All	**In the Name of Christ. Amen.**

Station Five

SENTENCE

Happy are those whose strength is in you – happy the pilgrims inspired by you. As they go through the valley they make it a place of springs.

From Psalm 84

READING

We give you thanks, most gracious God, for the beauty of the earth and sea, for the riches of mountains, plains, and rivers; for the song of the birds and the loveliness of flowers. We praise you for these good gifts, and pray that we may safeguard them for our prosperity. Grant that we may grow in our grateful enjoyment of your abundant creation; to the honour and glory of your Name, now and forever.   Amen.

PSALM

O Lord our governor,
How exalted is your name in all the world!
Out of the mouths of infants and children
Your majesty is praised above the heavens.
You have set us a stronghold against your adversaries,
To quell the enemy and the avenger.
When I consider your heavens, the work of your fingers,
The moon and the stars you have set in their courses,
What is man that you should be mindful of him?
The son of man that you should seek him out?
You have made him but little lower than the angels;

HOLY WELL STATIONS: FIVE

You adorn him with glory and honour;
You give him mastery over the works of your hands
You put all things under his feet
All sheep and oxen,
Even the wild beasts of the field,
The birds of the air, the fish of the sea,
And whatsoever walks in the paths of the sea.
O Lord our governor,
How exalted is your name in all the world!

Psalm 8

President   Let us know, let us press on to know the
Lord.

All   **His going forth is as sure as the dawn;
he will come to us as the showers, as the
spring rains that water the earth.**

Hosea 6.3

President   Let us go forth in peace.

All   **In the Name of Christ.   Amen.**

Station Six

SENTENCE

Tremble O earth at the presence of the Lord, at the presence
of the God of Jacob, who turns the rock into a pool of water,
the flint into a spring of water.

From Psalm 114

READING

I consider that the sufferings of this present time are not
worth comparing with the glory about to be revealed to us.
For the creation waits with eager longing for the revealing
of the children of God. For the creation was subjected to
futility, not of its own will but by the will of the one who
subjected it, in hope that the creation itself will be set free
from its bondage to decay and will obtain the freedom of
the glory of the children of God. We know that the whole
creation has been groaning in labour pains until now; and
not only the creation but we ourselves, who have the first
fruits of the Spirit, groan inwardly while we wait for adoption,
the redemption of our bodies.

Romans 8.18–23

PSALM

Sing to the Lord a new song;
Sing to the Lord all the whole earth.
Sing to the Lord and bless his name;
Proclaim the good news of his salvation from day to day.

Declare his glory among the nations
And his wonders among all peoples.
For great is the Lord and greatly to be praised;
He is more to be feared than all gods.
As for all the gods of the nations, they are but idols;
But it is the Lord who made the heavens.
Oh, the majesty and magnificence of his presence!
Oh, the power and the splendour of his sanctuary!
Ascribe to the Lord, you families of the peoples;
Ascribe to the Lord honour and power.
Ascribe to the Lord the honour due his name;
Bring offerings and come into his courts.
Worship the Lord in the beauty of holiness;
Let the whole earth tremble before him.
Tell it out among the nations; 'The Lord is king!
He has made the world so firm that it cannot be moved;
He will judge the peoples with equity.'
Let the heavens rejoice, and let the earth be glad;
Let the sea thunder and all that is in it;
Let the field be joyful and all that is therein.
Then shall all the trees of the wood shout for joy
Before the Lord when he comes,
When he comes to judge the earth.
He will judge the world with righteousness
And the peoples with his truth.

Psalm 96

PRAYER

May none of God's wonderful works keep silence, night or
morning. Bright stars, high mountains, the depths of the

HOLY WELLS

seas, sources of rushing rivers, holy wells; may all these break into song as we sing to Father, Son and Holy Spirit. May all the Angels in the heavens reply: Amen, Amen, Amen.

Anonymous, third–sixth century

President	Make me know the way I should walk.
All	**To you I lift up my soul.**
	Psalm 43
President	Let us go forth in peace.
All	**In the Name of Christ. Amen.**

Station Seven

SENTENCE

Build cairns to mark your way, set up signposts; make sure of the road, the path which you will tread.

Jeremiah 31.21

READING

Then Jesus came from Galilee to John at the Jordan, to be baptized by him. John would have prevented him saying, 'I need to be baptized by you, and do you come to me?' But Jesus answered him, 'Let it be so now; for it is proper for us in this way to fulfil all righteousness.' Then he consented. And when Jesus had been baptized, just as he came up from the water, suddenly the heavens were opened to him and he saw the Spirit of God descending like a dove and alighting on him. And a voice from heaven said, 'This is my Son, the Beloved, with whom I am well pleased.'

Matthew 3.13–17

PSALM

Bless the Lord, O my soul,
O Lord my God, how excellent is your greatness!
You are clothed with majesty and splendour.
You wrap yourself with light as with a cloak,
And spread out the heavens like a curtain.
You lay the beams of your chambers in the waters above;
You make the clouds your chariot;
You ride on the winds of the wind.

HOLY WELLS

You make the winds your messengers
And flames of fire your servants.
You have set the earth upon its foundations,
So that it never shall move at any time.
You covered it with the deep as with a mantel;
The waters stood higher than the mountains.
At your rebuke they fled;
At the voice of your thunder they hastened away.
They went up into the hills and down to the valleys
beneath,
To the places you had appointed for them.
You set the limits that they should not pass;
They shall not again cover the earth.
You send the springs into the valleys;
They flow between the mountains.
All the beasts of the field drink their fill from them,
And the wild asses quench their thirst.
Beside them the birds of the air make their nests
And sing among the branches.
You water the mountains from your dwelling on high;
The earth is fully satisfied by the fruit of your works.
You make grass grow for flock and herds
And plants to serve mankind;
That they may bring forth food from the earth,
And wine to gladden their hearts,
Oil to make a cheerful countenance,
And bread to strengthen the heart.
The trees of the Lord are full of sap,
The cedars of Lebanon which he planted,
In which the birds build their nests,
And in whose tops the stork makes his dwelling.

HOLY WELL STATIONS: SEVEN

The high hills are a refuge for the mountain goats,
And the stony cliffs for the rock badgers.
You appointed the moon to mark the seasons,
And the sun knows the time of its setting.
I will sing to the Lord as long as I live,
I will praise my God while I have my being.
Psalm 104.1–20, 34

PRAYER

O Gracious and Holy Father, give us wisdom to perceive
thee, diligence to seek thee, patience to wait for thee, eyes
to behold thee, a heart to meditate upon thee; through the
power of the Spirit of Jesus Christ our Lord.
Amen.

President   Let us go forth in peace.
All   **In the Name of Christ.   Amen.**

and this our life exempt from public haunt
Finds tongues in trees,
Books in the running brooks,
Sermons in stones
And good in everything.
Shakespeare, *As You Like It*

Station Eight

SENTENCE

The Lord says: 'I will guide them to streams of water by a level path where they will not stumble, for I am a father to my people.'
Isaiah 49.10

READING

A Samaritan woman came to draw water, and Jesus said to her, 'Give me a drink' (his disciples had gone to the city to buy food). The Samaritan woman said to him, 'How is it that you, a Jew, ask a drink of me, a woman of Samaria?' (Jews do not share things in common with Samaritans). Jesus answered her, 'If you knew the gift of God, and who it is that is saying to you, "Give me a drink", you would have asked him and he would have given you living water.' The woman said to him, 'Sir, you have no bucket, and the well is deep. Where do you get that living water? Are you greater than our ancestor Jacob, who gave us the well, and with his sons and his flocks drank from it?' Jesus said to her, 'Everyone who drinks of this water will be thirsty again, but those who drink of the water that I will give them will never be thirsty. The water that I will give will become in them a spring of water gushing up to eternal life.' The woman said to him, 'Sir, give me this water, so that I may never be thirsty or have to come here to draw water.'
John 4.7–15

HOLY WELL STATIONS: EIGHT

PSALM

The earth is the Lord's and all that is in it,
The world and all who dwell therein.
For it is he who founded it upon the seas
And made it firm upon the rivers of the deep
'Who can ascend the hill of the Lord?
And who can stand in his holy place?'
Those who have clean hands and a pure heart,
Who have not pledged themselves to falsehood,
Nor sworn by what is a fraud.
They shall receive a blessing from the Lord
And a just reward from the God of their salvation
Such is the generation of those who seek him,
Of those who seek your face, O God of Jacob.
Lift up your heads, O gates;
Lift them high, O everlasting doors;
And the King of glory shall come in.
'Who is the King of glory?'
'The Lord, strong and mighty,
The Lord, mighty in battle.'
Lift up your heads, O gates;
Lift them high, O everlasting doors;
And the King of glory shall come in.
'Who is he, this King of glory?'
'The Lord of hosts,
He is the King of glory.'
Psalm 24

HOLY WELLS

The shelter of Mary Mother
Be nigh my hands and my feet
To go out to the well
And to bring me safely home,
And to bring me safely home.
May warrior Michael aid me,
May Brigit calm preserve me,
May sweet Brianag give me light,
And Mary pure be near me,
And Mary pure be near me.

Carmina Gadelica 111, 169

When the shadows fall upon hill and glen;
And the bird-music is mute;
When the silken dark is a friend;
And the river sings to the stars;
Ask yourself sister,
Ask yourself, brother,
The question you alone have power
To answer:
O King and Saviour of all,
What is your gift to me?
And do I use it to your pleasing?

(pause)

President	Let us go forth in peace.
All	**In the Name of Christ. Amen.**

Station Nine

SENTENCE

The presence of the Incarnate Word penetrates like a universal element. It shines at the heart of all things.

Teilhard de Chardin

READING

O Father, give the spirit the power to climb
to the fountain of all light, and be purified.
Break through the mist of earth, the weight of the clod,
shine forth in splendour, Thou that art calm weather,
and quiet resting place for faithful souls.
To see thee is the end and the beginning,
Thou carriest us, and thou dost go before,
Thou art the journey, and the journey's end.

Boethius

PSALM

Sing to the Lord a new song;
Sing to the Lord all the whole earth.
Sing to the Lord and bless his name;
Proclaim the good news of his salvation from day to day.
Declare his glory among the nations
And his wonders among all peoples.
For great is the Lord and greatly to be praised;
He is more to be feared than all gods.
As for all the gods of the nations, they are but idols;
But it is the Lord who made the heavens.
O the majesty and magnificence of his presence!
O the power and the splendour of his sanctuary!

61

HOLY WELLS

Ascribe to the Lord, you families of the peoples;
Ascribe to the Lord honour and power.
Ascribe to the Lord the honour due his name;
Bring offerings and come into his courts.
Worship the Lord in the beauty of holiness;
Let the whole earth tremble before him.
Tell it out among the nations: 'The Lord is king!
He has made the world so firm that it cannot be moved;
He will judge the peoples with equity.'
Let the heavens rejoice, and let the earth be glad;
Let the sea thunder and all that is in it;
Let the field be joyful and all that is therein.
Then shall all the trees of the wood shout for joy
Before the Lord when he comes,
When he comes to judge the earth.
He will judge the world with righteousness
And the peoples with his truth.

Psalm 96

PRAYER

O God of unchangeable power and eternal light, look favourably on thy whole creation, that wonderful and sacred mystery, and by thy contrivance carry out the work of our true healing, and let the whole world feel and see that things which were cast down are being raised up, and things which had grown old are being made new, and all things are returning to perfection through Christ from whom they took their origin; to whom be all honour and glory.   Amen.

A Welsh Pilgrim's Manual

President   Let us go forth in peace.
All   **In the Name of Christ.   Amen.**

Station Ten

SENTENCE

Above all else guard your heart, for it is the wellspring of life.
Proverbs 4.23

MEDITATION EXERCISE

Find everything
In prayer
Which is fragrance
And food,
A home,
A shield,
A tonic.
Recall the reasons
Of your prayer;
The moments of despair;
The days of glad thanksgiving;
The times of stillness ....
Presence ....
Adoration ....
Love God the Creator;
Love the Cosmic Christ;
Remain in love.

Recapture and relive
The times you have felt
Loved;
Cared for; and treasured ....

HOLY WELLS

And see yourself going out ....
In Love ....
To friends
To those in need
And to every living creature.
Obtain peace and healing from your roots in nature.
Recall what happens
When you are in harmony
With earth and sky,
With rocks, sea, wind ....

Birds, animals, the
Creatures of the sea
And nature's many moods
And the seasons of the year.
We seek the Source of
Refreshment,
Sustenance,
And healing;
That our spirit, like our bodies
Are constantly in need of ....
We seek to be made whole
In solitude and silence ....
So now we seek to silence
Word and thought
By being conscious of the sounds
Around us ....
Or the sensation of the body ....
Of the breathing ....
We are energized by
LOVE.

HOLY WELL STATIONS: TEN

PRAYER

Lord Jesus Christ,
The world's true sun,
Ever rising, never setting,
Whose life-giving warmth
Engenders, preserves,
Nourishes and gladdens
All things in heaven and on earth;
Shine in my soul, I pray,
Scatter the night of sin,
And the clouds of error.
Blaze within me,
That I may go my way without stumbling,
Taking no part in the shameful deeds
Of those who walk in the dark;
But all my life long walking as one native to the light.
Amen.

Come Jesus Christ, King of the Elements,
Lead us as we walk with you
That the earth may be healed.

Farewell to you, O Holy Wells,
May your blessings with us remain;
And may His uncreated energy,
His grace, not part from us
Till we come this way again.
Amen.

Theophony

The words of the mouth are as deep waters and the wellsprings of wisdom as a flowing brook.
Proverbs 18.4 (KJV)

Running throughout the music of jazz is the *cantus firmus* (the 'firmsong'); the central melody around which other countermelodies are played. This is true too of classical music, in Bach's first 'cello suite there is a single theme running through it, which draws the listener within itself.

To hear it is to be ushered into the presence of God; it is polyphony, a simultaneous sounding of many interweaving melodies. It could be said that the Supreme Being – God – is a polyphony of Father/Creator, Son and Holy Spirit; a theophony, the Sound of God.

The Primal Sound of the Creator acting through the Cosmic Christ, is the Sound of Creation enabled by the Holy Spirit, the wavelength of God. We are attuned to the vibration of Creation in stillness; listening with the ear of the heart to the sound of the shimmering of eternity in time. God is the essence, the driver of the uncreated energy that is within and through music's vibration. The Sound of the Supreme Being.

THEOPHONY

This explanation, this Word is God,
In the eternal Now.
The I Am that I AM.
Wisdom, the breath of the power of God an emanation of
the power of the Almighty.

> Listen to the Breath of God.
> Listen to the Breath of Life.
> O that today you would listen to that
> Voice!

Lord, speak to me, that I may speak in living echoes of thy
tone.
Frances Ridley Havergal, hymn

HOLY WELLS

In the Beginning was
Silence,
And out of the silence came
Sound,
And out of the sound came the
Word,
And the word was
Vibration,
Which took
Shape,
In the alphabet of
Creation.
Out of no-thing
God spoke the
Word,
Which became
Matter,
The order and substance of
Cosmos.
Thus through the
Word made flesh,
All that is created out of silence,
Resonates
And returns toward the still, silent
Mystery of God
Before which all words ultimately fail.
Brendanus Scotus

THEOPHONY

God is with me

No matter how it may seem, God is in every situation, in every place.

I can be with Him here and rest myself in this truth.

As I listen to the sounds of creation, the wind in the trees, the birdsong all around me, the buzzing of bees, the whispering of grasses, the humming of insects; I know that God is present. Peace fills my mind and heart. I trust and know that everything is working for good.

God's energy is my strength. God is with me in all that I do and I am assured that all the details of every situation are being taken care of perfectly.

It does not matter what my need may be, God is with me in all ways. I turn my attention to God and lean trustingly on divine love and wisdom. With Him there is always a way and He is working in and through all things bringing about that which is right for my highest good.

All is well. Nothing is too daunting, for I have God's instant and constant support.

Amen.

HOLY WELLS

O Thou, who art the Perfection of Love, Harmony and Beauty.

The Lord of Heaven and Earth, open our hearts, so that we may hear Thy Voice,

which constantly cometh from within;

Disclose to us, Thy Divine Light, which is hidden in our souls,

that we may know and understand life better.

Most merciful and compassionate God, give us Thy great goodness;

Teach us Thy loving forgiveness;

Raise us above the distinctions and differences which divide humanity;

Send us the Peace of Thy Holy Spirit and unite us all in the I AM,

Thy Perfect Being, through Jesus Christ, our Lord.

Amen.

O flaming Mountain, O chosen Sun, O full Moon,
O bottomless Well, O unattainable Height,
O Brightness beyond compare, O Wisdom without
measure,
O Mercy unsurpassed, O Might irresistible,
O Crown of all glory: your lowly creature sings your
praises.
Mechthild of Magdeburg, 1210–82

THEOPHONY

River of God

Contemplation is the experience
Of God's love for us.
It is hidden and mystical.
God's love is like an
Underground river.
There is only One river and
We are many wells drawing living water from it.
This river passes through many religions
And each one claims it for its own;
But there is only One river ....
The Cosmic Christ which connects
All persons in the context of
Mystical experience.

Brendanus Scotus

Further Reading

As mentioned in the Foreword, this book is essentially a prayer book. It is not a history book, an antiquarian or a topographic guide.

There are a good number of books already published which would be of great value to anyone wishing to find a useful guide to assist in their quest. The ones listed below cover most of the places in the British Isles where holy wells are to be found. On modern maps the well sites are often unclear; whereas large scale maps can be a great help. It is best to find first or second edition Ordnance Survey maps.

If the site of the holy well is not already known (and a great deal are), then the following books will prove to be of tremendous help.

Bord, Janet and Colin, 1986, *Sacred Waters: Holy Wells and Water Lore in Britain and Ireland*, Granada Publishing.

Bord, Janet, 2008, *Holy Wells in Britain: A Guide*, Heart of Albion Press.

Bord, Janet, 2006, *Cures and Curses – Ritual and Cult at Holy Wells*, Heart of Albion Press.

Broadhurst, Paul, 1988, *Secret Shrines: In Search of the Old Holy Wells of Cornwall*, Paul Broadhurst.

FURTHER READING

Davis, Paul, 2003, *Sacred Springs: In Search of the Holy Wells and Spas of Wales*, Blorenge Books.

Harte, Jeremy, 2008, *English Holy Wells: A Sourcebook*, Heart of Albion Press.

Jones, Francis, 1954, *The Holy Wells of Wales*, University of Wales Press, facsimile reissue 1992.

MacLeod, Finlay, 2000, *The Healing Wells of the Western Isles*, Acair.

Miller, Joyce, 2000, *Myth and Magic: Scotland's Ancient Beliefs and Sacred Places*, Goblins Head.

Morris, Ruth and Frank, 1982, *Scottish Healing Wells: Healing, Holy, Wishing and Fairy Wells of the Mainland of Scotland*, The Alethea Press.

O'Malley, Brendan, 1981, *The Animals of St Gregory*, Paulinus Press.

— *A Pilgrim's Manual: St David's*, 1985, Paulinus Press.

— *A Welsh Pilgrim's Manual*, 1989, Gomer Press.

— *Pilgrim Guide: St David's*, 1997, Canterbury Press.

— *God at Every Gate*, 1997, Canterbury Press.

— *Celtic Blessings*, 1998, Canterbury Press.

— *A Celtic Eucharist*, 2002, Canterbury Press.

— *A Celtic Primer*, 2002, Canterbury Press.

— *Lord of Creation*, 2005, Canterbury Press.

— 'The Holy Wells of Pembrokeshire and their Associated Native Saints (excluding St David's)', unpublished thesis, 2005, University of Wales, Lampeter.

HOLY WELLS

Quiller-Couch, M. and L., 1894, *Ancient and Holy Wells of Cornwall*, Chas J. Clark.

Rattue, James, 1995, *The Living Stream: Holy Wells in Historical Context*, The Boydell Press.

Trier, Julie, 2004, 'A Study of Holy Wells in Pembrokeshire Including those of Our Lady and of St David and their Possible Association with Pilgrimage Routes to St David's', unpublished thesis, University of Wales, Lampeter.

Trubshaw, Bob, 2005 *Sacred Places: Prehistory and Popular Imagination*, Heart of Albion.

Yelton, Michael, 2006, *Alfred Hope Patten and the Shrine of Our Lady of Walsingham*, Canterbury Press.

Zaluckj, Sarah and John, 2006, *The Celtic Christian Sites of the Central and Southern Marches*, Logaston Press.

Gazetteer

I have selected holy wells which best fit with the prayer book; and I am grateful to Janet Bord for permission to cull the wells described in this list from her excellent book, *Holy Wells in Britain – A Guide*, which incidentally makes a wonderful companion to this prayer book. The letters (JB) refer to direct quotes from Janet Bord. Also listed are OS map references. For those seeking further information, there are many holy well sources to be found on 'The Living Spring' website:

(http://people.bath.ac.uk/liskmj/living-spring/sourcearchive/front.htm);

and in two issues of the online journal 'Living Spring':

(http://people.bath.ac.uk/liskmj/living-spring/journal/home.htm).

ENGLAND

Cornwall

Madron Holy Well – just north of the village of Madron in Cornwall, the well has long been known for its healing powers. Visitors leave pieces of cloth tied to the tree according to traditional custom at healing wells. Nearby are the remains of a simple twelfth-century chapel dedicated to St Madern. SW445327.

St Anne's Well, Whitstone – in the churchyard of Whitstone Church. SX263986.

St Cleer's Well, St Cleer – in the village of St Cleer in the centre of the village. SX249683.

St Clether's Well, St Clether – a footpath leads to the well from behind the church. SA202846.

St Keyne's Well, St Keyne – beside a lane half a mile south east of St Keyne Church, at a minor junction. SX248603.

St Neot's Well, St Neot – on the southern edge of Bodmin Moor, just outside the village and along the valley of St Neot River. SX183680.

Southam Holy Well – lying in the Stowe river valley, the well is a ten-minute walk west of Southam town centre along a signposted path from St James' Church. The water is reputed to be effective in curing eye problems. SP410618.

Devon

St Brannoc's Well, Braunton – a stone-edged pool in the grounds of St Brannoc's Church. The entrance is opposite Frog Lane: take the lower lane down to the church. SS487374.

Ladywell, Pilton – in a lane behind Pilton Parish Church (north-west corner of churchyard). *'The water has been used for baptism and healing' (JB)*. SS557341.

St Nectan's Well, Welcombe – a beautiful well, the water often used for baptisms. Ten miles north of Bude. SS228184.

GAZETTEER

Somerset

St Agnes' Well, Cothelstone – a romantic well and attractive in its own right. Known as 'lovers well'. ST184318.

St Andrew's Well, Wells – a well among other wells in the aptly named city. *'A pool in front of the Cathedral is also known as the holy well of St Andrew' (JB)*. ST552458.

Chalice Well, Glastonbury – a more modern well than the norm, located in a garden from which water flows through the garden. Atmospheric location in the care of the Chalice Well Trust at the foot of the Tor. ST507385.

St Decuman's Well, Watchet – the well is close to the church at St Decuman's to the west of Watchet, which is along the coast six miles south-east of Minehead. From the church follow the lane downhill (to the west) and the well is through a gate on the right. ST064427.

St Joseph's Well, Glastonbury – the well is below the crypt of the Lady Chapel in Glastonbury Abbey. The *well* can be seen through a grille. In the centre of the town. ST501388.

Berkshire

St Anne's Well, Caversham – located to the north of Reading, St Anne's well is at the top of Priest Hill next to the junction with St Anne's Road, across from Caversham Bridge over the River Thames. The well is surrounded by a grille, and is now dry. *'This well has a plaque placed on it stating that it was "The holy well of St Anne, the healing waters of which brought many pilgrims to Caversham in the Middle Ages"' (JB)*. SU712750.

Ladywell, Speen – a wishing well by tradition. Speen is to the north-west of Newbury, by the A4. The Ladywell is approximately 50 yards from the graveyard of the Church of St Mary the Virgin, to which a grassy track leads from the Bath road. A short distance down the track a turning to the right leads to the Ladywell. SU455680.

Dorset

St Augustine's Well, Cerne Abbas – the village of Cerne Abbas is north of Dorchester, and the well is to the north of the church near the ruined abbey. Walk along the street towards the abbey with the church on your right, and at the abbey entrance go through the gate on the right; the path to the well is signposted. *'An historic holy well with many stories concerning its provenance. Reputed to be a fertility and healing well, and efficacious in healing sore eyes and various other maladies. Recent history tells that Augustine's well is also a wishing well' (JB).* ST666014.

Lady's Well, Hermitage – park by St Mary's Church and follow the footpath signposted to Lyons Hill – over the bridge, through a wood; halfway across the field turn right to the bottom corner of the wood. The well will be found just inside. Hermitage was, as its name indicated, home to a succession of hermits in the fourteenth to fifteenth centuries. ST651068.

St Wite's Well, Morcombelake – the well is found halfway between Bridport and Lyme Regis, a short distance south of Morcombelake, across the A35. The lane to take off the main road is Ship Knapp Lane and it has two entrances. Drive a short distance up the lane and the well is signposted to the left. There is a small parking space by the lane. Follow the track across the field on foot and the well is shortly found in a small enclosure beside the track on the right hand side. *'Water from the well was once used to cure sore eyes, and in order for it to be effective, they had to be bathed at first light. Bent pins were thrown into the well as a votive offering, and the supplicant would also say: "Holy well, holy well, take my gift and cast a spell"' (JB).* SY399938.

Hampshire

Holy Well, Sopley – across the river from the church, the well is beside the gateway to the Bible College on the B3347. *'Red brick steps lead down to a basin into which water trickles from an animal's head. A plaque above has a figure of Christ and the Alpha and Omega signs. This well has mistakenly been given the name of St Michael's well, based solely on the church dedication' (JB).* SZ157969.

Iron's Well (or Lepers' Well), Fritham – the chalybeate water was once used to treat leprosy, and later to cure mangy dogs. The well is north-east of Eyeworth Pond which is north-west of Fritham; there is a car park at the pond. SU229147.

Wiltshire

Daniel's Well, Malmesbury – beside the River Avon, on the west side of Malmesbury, and reached by a footpath from the town centre – a walk down alleys and steps taking only a few minutes. The route can be easily found by obtaining a walks leaflet from the Information Centre. Daniel's Well is named after an abbot of Malmesbury Abbey who *'regularly immersed himself in its water to wash away his sins'* ('Immersion', in Janet Bord, *Cures and Curses*). ST931872.

London

St Mary's Well, Willesden – inside St Mary's Church, Neasden Lane, Willesden (London NW10 2TS), which is just off the Neasden Lane/High Road roundabout. There is car parking beside the Parish Centre. The nearest underground station is Neasden on the Jubilee Line. The church is open daily. An interesting history relates more than one holy well at this location: *'From late Victorian times a pond in the vicarage garden was regarded as a holy well and its water was used for healing purposes. However a spring was recently discovered in the old boiler-house (a former family vault) below ground level, and the water is now pumped up into the church, where it can be obtained from a free-standing dispenser which has a tap and a large bowl. People come to the church to obtain supplies of the water for healing purposes, and at least five miraculous cures have been claimed in recent times'* (JB).

Kent

The Black Prince's Well, Harbledown – Harbledown is west of Canterbury, and the well is to be found at the west end of the grounds behind the old leper hospital. Travelling west through Harbledown, turn left up Summer Hill, then go down Church Hill, and St Nicholas Hospital and Church are on the left. The well is on the left-hand side of the path inside the gate. *'This well is named after Edward, Prince of Wales, eldest son of Edward III, known as the Black Prince, who is said to have sent for water from the well during his last illness in 1376. He may have suffered from a mild form of leprosy and the well water was believed to help that condition, as well as being good for eye complaints'* (JB). TR129581.

St Edith's Well, Kemsing – attractive keyhole-shaped well with steps leading down to the water. The well is in its own garden, near The Bell Inn in the centre of the village of Kemsing, three miles north-east of Sevenoaks. TQ555587.

St Margaret's Well, Broomfield – located near the church, indicated by a wooden cross. *'Well-dressing now takes place here on the Sunday nearest to St Margaret's Day (20 July)' (JB).* TQ839525.

Surrey

St Anne's Well (Nuns Well), St Anne's Hill, Chertsey – there was once a chapel dedicated to St Anne close by the well, and both were probably once much visited by pilgrims. This is an 'eye well' for the healing of eye diseases. On the north side of St Anne's Hill, a mile north-west of Chertsey. Can be found by following the Nature Trail. TQ028676.

Mag's Well (or Meg's Well), Mugswell – located in the garden of the Well House pub in Chipstead Lane, it now looks like a traditional wishing well, but was once famed for healing many complaints. The name may originally have been St Margaret's Well. TQ258553.

St Mary the Virgin's Well, Dunsfold – an attractive well with canopy designed by W. D. Caroe. Tradition tells of numerous visions of the Blessed Virgin Mary by visiting pilgrims. It is an 'eye well'. The water is used for baptisms in the church. Located close to Dunsfold Church, eight miles south of Guildford. A signposted footpath leads downhill from the church to the well. SU997363.

Sussex

Bone Well, Willingdon – located beside the road through the village. Notable for being decorated with cows' knuckle bones set in flint. TQ88021.

Spring at Fulking, West Sussex – the Victorian well-house beside the village street carries a text from Psalm 104: 'He sendeth springs into the valleys which run among the hills. O that men would praise the Lord for his goodness' TQ247113.

Bedfordshire

Holy Well, Stevington – the well is under an arch in the churchyard wall surrounding the Church of St Mary, which has Saxon stonework in part of the tower. Located in the village of Stevington, four miles north-west of Bedford. Turn left on coming out of the church gate and follow for a few yards. The well is in the churchyard wall. SP991536.

Buckinghamshire

Schorne Well, North Marston – the well originally had four steps down into the water, but by the 1990s it was in a bad state of repair with only a pump and a structure like a coal bunker. The villagers have since restored the well, erecting a triangular oak building with a tiled roof, a brick floor, and a new pump and trough. There was a service of blessing in May 2005. Located in the village of North Marston, five miles north of Aylesbury. The well is in Schorne Lane off Church Street, about 150 yards from St Mary's Church. Signposted. The well's name commemorates Sir John Schorne, rector from 1290 to 1314, and it was used as a healing well, especially for ague and gout. In addition, *'a glass of the water drunk at night was said to cure any cold ere daybreak' (JB)*. SP777225.

Gloucestershire

St Anthony's Well, Forest of Dean – the well is hidden in the woods north of Cinderford (it can be reached by lanes and paths from Cinderford and Flaxley). From the north on the A4136, travelling towards Monmouth; after Mitcheldean, on reaching the Plump Hill sign, take the lane to the left (Jubilee Road) and drive for about two miles until a Forestry Commission sign is reached. Park here and walk the rest of the way. Keeping right past the industrial area, the track then continues straight ahead towards the trees. Here is a large pool, and the well is uphill to the right. The water flows down into the pool so investigate the streams flowing into the pool until you find the well. *'This is an impressive well in an unusual location. It is not in a village, beside a lane, or close to a church – instead it is hidden away in a fine beech wood, seemingly far from human habitation, and it is well worth seeking out' (JB)*. SO670158.

St Kenelm's Well, Winchcombe – Winchcombe is five miles north-east of Cheltenham, and the well is a mile east of the town. Approaching from Winchcombe along the lane that leads to Guiting Power, a mile out of town there is a farm on the left, with space to park by the roadside. A footpath sign points across a field uphill to the left, but there is no mention of the well. Having crossed the field, a stile will be reached; and having walked straight across the next field there is another stile. From here the well building can be seen to the left. *'Kenelm was a son of Coenwulf, King of Mercia in the ninth century; buried at Winchcombe Abbey. From the tenth century Kenelm came to be regarded as a martyr and a saint and legends grew around him. His shrine at Winchcombe was a focus for pilgrimage before the Reformation, and many miracles were said to have been performed there' (JB)*. SP043278.

Herefordshire

St Clodock's Well, Clodock – a few minutes' walk from St Clawdog's Church at Clodock, on the other side of the river. There is a tradition that the original site of the church was on the same side as the well and closer to it. Clodock is in the remote west of the county, 15 miles south-west of Hereford. To reach the well from the church, pass the Cornewell Arms on the left, cross the river, and take a footpath to the right beside the river. The well is on the left before the house is reached. It is close to the river and is submerged when the river floods. SO326273.

Holy Well, Garway – the original church at Garway was a Knights Templar foundation. The holy well is a spring located just outside the churchyard at the south-east corner. The water flows from a spout into a small pool in the churchyard, though it is sometimes dry. SO455224.

Hertfordshire

Holy Well, St Albans – in the centre of St Albans, on Holywell Hill, turn left down Belmont Hill then turn right down De Tany Court. Shortly you will see a garden containing a fenced enclosure, in the centre of which is a low wall forming a square, which is the site of the well. TL146067.

Northamptonshire

Becket's Well, Northampton – the well has been restored and murals by local schoolchildren depicting the life of St Thomas Becket have been installed there. It can be found on Bedford Road. Fifty yards from the Bedford Road/Victoria Promenade/Derngate/Cheyne Walk crossroads. SP761602.

Oxfordshire

Lady Well, Wilcote – walk from Wilcote Church along an avenue of trees. It is an evocative place and gives a pleasant experience of pilgrimage. Wilcote is between Fristock and North Leigh, north-east of Witney. From Wilcote Church, take the footpath heading south-east towards North Leigh, and the well will be seen at the end of the avenue of ancient trees. SP374147.

St Margaret's Well, Binsey – best approached from the west, along the A420 into Oxford from Botley. In New Botley/Osney follow the lane north to Binsey and keep on this lane until the end, where the church is situated with the well outside the west end. *'Although so close to Oxford, Binsey Church and well are in a rural setting in meadowland; although sadly now close to the busy A34. There is evidence that both well and church still receive many pilgrims, and Binsey is an oasis of calm' (JB).* SP485080.

Warwickshire

Berks Well, Berkswell – the 'well' is a stone tank sixteen feet square and five feet deep, possibly used for baptism by immersion. It was restored in the nineteenth century.

Berkswell is five miles west of Coventry and the well is to the south of the church outside the main gate and beside a footpath. *'Berk is thought to derive from the personal name Beorcol, and the place name was given as Berchewelle in the eleventh-century Doomsday Book' (JB)*. SP244790.

Rowton's Well, Sutton Park – the water of Rowton's Well was said to have medicinal properties. The other named wells are Keeper's Well and Druid's Well (or St Mary's Well). Sutton Park is to the north-west of Sutton Coldfield. There are many points of access, with car parks and footpaths. Rowton's Well is a mile north-east of the car park at Banners Gate. SP093965. Keeper's Well is on the feeder stream to Keeper's Pool; Druid's Well is on the south-west end of Bracebridge Pool.

Worcestershire

St Anne's Well – half a mile west of Great Malvern town centre and reached via a steep path which is signposted from the top of Church Street. SO772458.

Holy Well – the building dates from 1843 but the earliest written reference to the holy well is from 1558. As at St Anne's Well, the water can be sampled here. Located at a hairpin bend on Holy Well Road, Malvern Wells, to the south of Great Malvern. SO770423.

St Katherine's Well, Bredon Hill – *'There was once a medieval chapel close to this well, and excavation has revealed foundations. The spring water flows into a stone trough. It can be found on the steep north flank of the hill, directly below Parson's Folly, on the corner of a wood. After parking near*

Woolas Hall Farm a path leads past Woolas Hall and uphill to the right of the well. The stream seen on your left has the well as its source' (JB). SO953403.

St Kenelm's Well, Romsley – the rural oasis of the Clent Hills is located west of the M5 motorway, south of Dudley. The Church of St Kenelm is north-east of the village of Clent, and north-west of Romsley. There is car parking beside the lane, and a footpath leads from the east end of the church into a wooded valley where the well will easily be found. SO944807.

Cambridgeshire

Holy Well, Holywell – the well is easily found behind the church. *'Holywell, two miles south-east of St Ives, is mentioned in the* Doomsday Book, *as Haliewelle, so this well was important at least as far back as the eleventh century. During the 1980s well-dressing was introduced, a service of blessing the well and the church flower festival being held late in June to coincide with the patronal festival of St John the Baptist' (JB).* TL336707.

Holy Well, Longstanton – the well in the churchyard of the redundant St Michael's Church. Take the road to the Barracks and turn right down St Michael's Lane, beneath a big chestnut tree and protected by railings. TL403658.

Red Well, Knapwell – as its name suggests, Red Well is a chalybeate spring and was believed to have medicinal properties. Knapwell is seven miles north-west of Cambridge, and the well can be found in Boxworth Wood which is now the Overhall Grove Nature Reserve. At the north end of the village a track leads to the church, from where a footpath can be followed into the wood. Pass the information box and then take the path right into the woods. The well is due east of the church. TL337630.

Essex

St Peter's Well, West Mersea – this well was once attached to the lost priory of St Peter and St Paul, and was restored in 2000. Accessible by path from Coast Road. TM006124.

Lincolnshire

St John's Well, Bottesford – the well is protected by a Victorian stone well-house; the water is in a sunken stone trough. Located in a southern suburb of Scunthorpe, at the junction of Manor Road and Church Lane. SE898070.

Norfolk

Walsingham Wells – it was an important shrine before the Reformation, and has become a great shrine again since its restoration in the early twentieth century. There is the Anglican Shrine of Our Lady of Walsingham and a Catholic shrine nearby. Three separate holy wells can be visited, each with its own history. Location: the wells are in the Priory grounds, close to an archway. The grounds are open to the public at certain times of the day, with access from the village centre. A Sprinkling Service takes place daily at 2.30pm and plastic bottles stamped with the image of Our Lady of Walsingham may be purchased. Location: inside the Anglican Shrine in the centre of the village of Little Walsingham. Access is open to all. Just inside the main entrance steps lead down to the holy well under the reconstructed Holy House.

The Slipper Chapel, Catholic Shrine, is at Houghton St Giles, half a mile from Little Walsingham: there is a large car park. Both shrines are open to all faiths and more. Both shrines have their own websites.

St Walstan's Well, Bawburgh – a spring just below Bawburgh Church is the well that is depicted on the village sign, and is well cared for. St Walstan's feast is commemorated each year with a service held in the church plus a procession to the well for prayer. Located at Bawburgh, about five miles to the west of Norwich city centre. There is parking by the church gates. To reach the well do not enter the churchyard but continue along the lane and follow it round to the right, and the well can be seen in an area of grass and trees to the right beyond the house. TG153087.

St Withburga's Well, Dereham – Dereham is 15 miles west of Norwich and the well is easy to find in the churchyard of St Nicholas' Church on the west side of the town. TF986133.

Suffolk

The Lady's Well, Blythburgh – the structure is an arched shelter, a pillar on both sides, and two stone seats inside. There used to be brass cups chained to the shelter so that travellers could drink the water. The well is set into an earth bank beside the Blythburgh to Beccles road just before the turning to Blyford. TM450762.

Cheshire

St Chad's Well, Romiley – the well is accessible at all times. Since the late twentieth century well-dressing has taken place here annually to coincide with Chadkirk's Summer Festival at the end of July. Located on the Chadkirk Country Estate, south of Romiley (east of Stockport) to the east of the A627. If travelling from the south, turn right shortly after the two sharp bends. There is a car park to the left, and the well is then reached on foot. Either walk straight up the lane, past the chapel and past the farm; going uphill the well is found on the left. Or follow the Waymark circular walk round the estate grounds which also passes the chapel and well. SJ939904.

St Plegmund's Well, Plemstall – Plemstall is a hamlet in the parish of Mickle Trafford, two miles north-east of Chester. The well is beside Plemstall Lane which leads from the A56 to Plemstall Church. It is on the north side of the lane about 200 yards west of the church by a bridge, and is easy to miss among the foliage despite the large superstructure. SJ455701.

Derbyshire

St Anne's Well, Buxton – outside the Micrarium (the former Pump Room), at the bottom of the slopes, a sloping public garden in the centre of Buxton.

Leicestershire

Holy Well, Ab Kettleby – the water was believed to be good for rheumatism. To find the well, turn left off the main road into the village (from the south) then left into Church Lane. The pond is to the right; the well is on the left by the footpath. SK724229.

Nottinghamshire

St Catherine's Well, Newark – the spring now known as St Catherine's Well is close to the Civil War fortification. Known as the Queen's Source, by the River Devon; but it is in a cottage garden – so please do not trespass. SK90530.

Rutland

Wishing Well, Ashwell – the well is easily found on the west of the village, in a clump of trees where the Laugham road turns off the Oakham road. SK864137.

Shropshire

St Cuthbert's Well, Donington – this well had a reputation for curing sore eyes bathed with its water. It has a stone canopy and can be found in a wooded dell below St Cuthbert's Church. Donington is close to Albrighton, north-west of Wolverhampton, but not signposted; so if travelling along the A41 look for Rectory Road. SJ808045.

St Julian's Well, Ludlow – a small stone well-house, which is Grade II listed, covers this well which was originally a water supply in an Augustinian Friary. It can be found under a large tree in the middle of Livesey Road. SO518750.

St Milburga's Well, Stoke St Milburga – an 'eye-well'. The well was restored at the end of the last century. Located in Stoke St Milburga, six miles north-east of Ludlow, and the well is near the church. On entering the village from the south, head for the church but do not drive into the dead-end lane to the left that leads to the church entrance (with red post-box); keep going up the hill and round a sharp left hand bend, after which there is a wide entrance on the left, and immediately afterwards a rustic gate leading to the well. SO567823.

St Oswald's Well, Oswestry – on the west side of Oswestry. To find the well from the town centre go to the crossroads with traffic lights near the parish church and take the Trefonen road westwards, then turn second right into Oswald's Place and follow this road along Oswald's Well Lane. The well is on the left hand side, close to the road but hidden from view in a hollow with trees around. There is a plaque at the entrance, and the new housing close by has adopted the name Maserfield. SJ284293.

Staffordshire

St Chad's Well, Stowe, Lichfield – Stowe Church is to the north of Lichfield, on the northern edge of Stowe Pool, and the well is in the churchyard. SK122103.

Egg Well, Bradnop – Bradnop is two miles south-east of Leek and the well is a mile away, reached along lanes to the south. Follow the lane across the main road from Bradnop village; drive as far as the entrance to Middle Cliff Farm, park on the verge. Walk down the lane leading to Roost Hill Farm. The well building will be seen under the trees on the grass verge at the next junction, opposite the bungalow 'Fernleigh'. *'The egg well was probably one of those wells which straddles the line between healing well and simple spa' (JB)*. SK006541.

Cumbria

St Cuthbert's Well, Colton – set into a grassy bank below a remote hilltop church, the well was restored for the millennium. It is approached through a small circular-built enclosure and is lined with sandstone. A large stone above it is inscribed 'St Cuthbert's Well'. The water used to be used for baptisms in the church. The well can be found beside an ancient path leading uphill to the church (opposite church gate) at Colton, six miles north-east of Ulverston. SD318861.

St Helen's Well, Great Asby – once used for baptism at the nearby church. The well can be found on the north bank of the stream on the green at the centre of the village, just east of the church. NY682133.

St Kentigern's Well, Aspatria – in the churchyard to the north of the church can be found a small stone well-house built into a bank and approached by an open walled court, all now overgrown. The water was once used for baptisms. NY137420.

St Kentigern's Well or *St Mungo's Well, Caldbeck* – at Caldbeck the saint is depicted in a church window and his well is just outside the churchyard to the west end of the church below the stone bridge (steps down to the well) – a simple trough on the river bank. *'Kentigern Mungo (this well appears under both names) was a missionary Bishop in Strathclyde (i.e. Glasgow). He was educated by St Servan who gave him the name "Mungo" which means "dear friend". He travelled to Cumberland and then to Wales where he founded the monastery at St Asaph. Asaph was trained in the monastic life by St Kentigern Mungo and succeeded him as Bishop of the diocese of St Asaph, North Wales, in the sixth century' (JB).* NY325399.

St Mungo's Well, Bromfield – to be found immediately to the north of the church. There is a path from the churchyard. The water can be seen in the circular stone shaft about two feet below ground level. NY176470.

St Oswald's Well, Kirkoswald – Kirkoswald is nine miles north east of Penrith, and the church and its separate bell tower are at the south end of the village. There is room to park one car by the entrance gate on the B6413. *'The well consists of a stone and brick superstructure in which is a circular hole protected by a metal cover. When this is lifted, you can see down into the well. This can also be accessed more directly down some steps to the side. A metal cup on a chain is provided for easy access to the water' (JB)*. NY555409.

Durham

St Cuthbert's Well, Durham – little is known about this well below Durham Cathedral. It has a large sandstone surround with the inscription 'FONS: CUTHBERT (1600 OR 1660)'. St Cuthbert is closely linked with Durham, his grave, portable altar and seventh-century coffin are in the cathedral. Access to the well is difficult, down a steep path between the Cathedral and the River Wear. NZ272421.

Holy Well, Wolsingham – there is a large building like a little house over this well, now a listed building, and the water is used for religious purposes in a chapel which once stood nearby; but nothing seems to be known about its history. It is on the north side of the lane leading from the Inn at the north of the village to the hospital. NZ077378.

St Mary's Well, Gainford – located close to the church, this well once supplied water for baptism. To find it, go to the church on the village green, through the churchyard and down a steep path towards the river. The well is under the churchyard. The water flows into a stone trough and then away to the river. NZ169167.

St Oswald's Well, Durham – *'Situated just below the footpath leading from St Oswald's churchyard to Prebend's Bridge. Reached down a narrow steep footpath about 20 yards after entering the trees below the church tower. Today this well consists of a large cavern cut into the sandstone rock outcrop part way down the steep well-wooded banks of the Wear overlooking the Cathedral. A small rock ledge at the front of the cavern dams up a pool of water; the overflow pouring over the ledge and down to the river below'* (Laurence Hunt, 1987, Ancient, Healing and Holy Wells of County Durham, *source 7*).

Lancashire

Holy Well, Hollinshead, Tockholes – the well is about two miles south of Tockholes, just to the south of Blackburn. It is accessible by footpath from the Slipper Lowe picnic and car park area, which is reached from the lane south of Tockholes and is just under a mile north of the lane's junction with the A675 halfway between the Abbey Village and Belmont. Hollinshead Hall is signposted from the car park. Where the paths diverge (no sign at this point), go right downhill into the trees and see the low walls of the demolished hall, well-house on the left. Back at the car park the track through the gate also leads down to Hollinshead Hall (go left at the junction). SD663199.

Ladyewell, Fernyhalgh Lane, Fulwood – Located north of Preston. Leave the M6 motorway at Junction 32 (signed

Preston, Garstang) and at the roundabout follow the Preston sign, immediately getting in the left hand lane signposted: Longridge and Ribbleton. At the next small roundabout turn right. There are numerous Ladyewell signs along this route. Continue to the large roundabout and follow the Ladyewell sign. The road goes over the motorway and shortly after this take the right turn (again signposted to Ladyewell). Along this lane on the left is a car and coach park for the shrine just before the Catholic church, which was built because of its proximity to the well. *'The Catholic Marian Shrine centred on Ladyewell House has the holy well as its centrepiece. Pilgrims are always welcome at Ladyewell House where in addition to the well there is a chapel; a library; a room holding saints' relics; a Padre Pio memorial, and many other features of devotion. This place is a must for the devout pilgrim and is one of the most visited places of pilgrimage today'* (JB). SD557334.

St Patrick's Well, Heysham – the well, also known as Church Well, is set into the wall beside the entrance to the path to St Peter's churchyard. Almost certainly the well was given its dedication because of its proximity to St Patrick's Chapel, whose remains, with unusual rock-cut graves, lie only a few minutes' walk away to the north-west of St Peter's Church. SD411617.

St Thomas' Well, Windle – *'St Helen's Cemetery is now the location of this well, close to the stepped base and shaft of Windlesham Cross; which itself is close to the ruins of Gerard Chantry Chapel of St Thomas's, known locally as Windleshaw Abbey. There has been a Catholic burial ground here since the seventeenth century, and it is probable that the well is also at least that old. It is circular, six yards in diameter, twelve feet deep* and lined with stone. A name plate with "St Thomas's Well" and another with "1798" and "H.W.E." can be seen, the initials being that of William and Elizabeth Hill who owned the land when the well sides were raised. Windle is to the north-west of St Helens, and the Cemetery is south of the A580' (JB). SJ497969.

Northumberland

St Cuthbert's Well, Bellingham, also known as Cuddy's Well – 'The Saint was said to have discovered the spring by dowsing, and consecrated it. The water was used for baptism in the nearby church. The well is in a grassy lane just outside the churchyard wall' (JB). NY837833.

Lady Well, Holystone, also known as St Ninian's Well – in the eighteenth century it was St Paulinus's well. It seems to have taken its name of Lady Well from the nearby house of Benedictine nuns dedicated to St Mary the Virgin. Location: Holystone is seven miles west of Rothbury. The well is north of the village, reached by a short footpath from the village itself. NT952029.

Yorkshire East

St Helen's Well, Goodmanham – the water from the spring under an ancient elder tree flows into a shallow triangular pool which may have been used as a bath. However there appears to be no surviving history. It can be found in a wooded valley south of Goodmanham and is reached from the lane leading from Market-Weighton to South Dalton. A footpath to the left five hundred yards past the crossroads leads to the well which is close to the lane. SE891424.

HOLY WELLS

St Helen's Well, Great Hatfield, East Riding of Yorkshire – near the cemetery. It is also called Rag Well because pieces of clothing or lace would be dipped in the water and knotted on the hawthorn hedges as a thanksgiving for blessings to be received. TA188426.

St Helen's Well, Farnhill – Yorkshire has many wells dedicated to St Helen, several of which are worth visiting. At this one the water flows into a stone trough against a wall. Farnhill adjoins Kildwick four miles south-east of Skipton, and the well is near the junction to Low Bradley. SE005466.

St Hilda's Well, Hinderwell – Hinderwell is eight miles north-west of Whitby. *'This well, a simple stone structure at the end of a flight of steps behind the church, is a strangely atmospheric site. It used to be the custom for children to mix the well water with liquorice on Ascension Day, which was here known as Spanish Water Day' (JB).* NZ791170.

St John's Well, Harpham – Harpham is five miles south-west of Bridlington, and the well is beside a lane just to the east of the village; from the church, go to the crossroads in the centre and turn right. The well is signposted. *'The well is dedicated to St John of Beverley who was born in Harpham. He is said to have struck the ground with his staff whereupon a spring began to flow. St John's Well was said to never run dry, and according to William of Malmesbury it had power to subdue wild bulls and other savage beasts. The water was also said to be helpful in curing headaches and eye ailments. It is now scarcely visible inside the small stone well-house, though it can be heard if you throw in a coin' (JB).* TA095617.

GAZETTEER

Yorkshire North

St Cedd's, St Chad's and St Ovin's Wells, Lastingham – aside from the fact that this village has three holy wells, it is worth visiting anyway for the church and its unique eleventh-century crypt. All three wells are on the roadside within walking distance of the church. Lastingham is five miles north-west of Pickering; there is roadside parking close to the church which is open daily. SE728905.

Mary Magdalene Well, Spaunton – a spring flows into a small stone trough at this unspoilt rural well, and the name is carved on a stone above. Fragments of Saxon and thirteenth-century pottery have been found, suggesting it is an ancient well. It is tucked into a steep bank just below the lane leading west from Lastingham, just north of Spaunton, close to cottages by a junction. SE722904.

Yorkshire South and West

St James' Well, Midhopestones – 'This is South Yorkshire's best preserved holy well. A small square stone chamber protected by railings. Along with the nearby Potter's Well, it is decorated annually, and a blessing ceremony is held. To the south-east is St James' Chapel, rebuilt in 1705 on the site of an earlier chapel. Midhopestones is two miles north-west of Stocksbridge, and the well is in a field to the north of a track leading to Midhope Hall' (JB). SK234995.

Peace Well, Dore – in 1959 this well was restored. The first well-dressing took place in that year. The well is at the south-east corner of the village green in Dore (five miles south-west of Sheffield); also on the green is the King Egbert Stone which commemorates the proclamation of Egbert of Mercia as the first King of all England in AD 829. SK309811.

Town's Well, Hampole – a plaque near the well records that Richard Rolle lived close to this spot; on the south side of the village green at Hampole, six miles north-west of Doncaster. *'A Cistercian convent dedicated to St Mary was founded here in 1170, but there are no visible remains. Richard Rolle, a popular English mystical writer in the late Middle Ages, lived here as a hermit until his death in 1349. A local farmer had a dream in which he was requested to build a tomb for Rolle and by 1395 his body was located close to the high altar of the church, with miracles occurring and pilgrims coming to the shrine'* (JB). SE50510399.

WALES

Anglesey

Ffynnon Seiriol (St Seiriol's Well), Penmon – the well is close to the impressive priory church dating from the twelfth century. The other building is a fine stone dovecote, c. 1600, with a vaulted dome roof. The car park is opposite. Turn left at the dovecote-end of the car park and follow a short path to the well, above a former monastic fishpond. The well is clearly a bathing well also used for divination. Penmon is four miles north-east of Beaumaris. SH631808.

Ffynnon Wenfaen (St Gwenfaen's Well), Rhoscolyn – since the saint's name means 'white stone' the practice of throwing two white stones into the well as an offering may have evolved from it, though white quartz pebbles were also offered at other Welsh wells (see previous chapter on prayer stones). Rhoscolyn is five miles south of Holyhead, and the walk starts near the church where there is room to park. Take the track heading south-west for about half a mile, and turn right at the coastguard lookout; following the path for another half mile to the well. *'This well consists of a sunken square stone-built forecourt accessed by steps on the east side, and with four seats across the corners. This gives access to an open oblong chamber facing the steps, with the water flowing west under the enclosing wall, into an uncovered oblong bathing tank accessed at either end by steps. The water was once used to protect against mental problems, and it was noted in the eighteenth century that it was customary to throw in two white pebbles as an offering'* (JB). SH259755.

Carmarthenshire

St Anthony's Well and Ffynnon Fair (St Mary's Well), Llansteffan (Llanstephan) – about a mile from the church. Park near the church and walk down the road past the church itself which leads to the castle. At the car turning circle, walk straight on through the wood and along the cliff-top path to St Anthony's Bay. Follow the garden wall of the one house on the bay; the well is down some steps in the wall about 50 yards along. *'St Anthony's Well was a healing well, and later a wishing well. It is in a walled enclosure, with the water inside a pointed stone arch, and a narrow stone ledge at the back which was called "the offering shelf"'* (JB).

Ffynnon Deilo (St Teilo's Well), Llandeilo – in the early medieval period Llandeilo seems to have been a major centre of St Teilo's cult. The well is near the eastern end of the church, the water flowing into a twelve foot square alcove below the level of the raised churchyard. Although this was a town water supply for centuries, its proximity to the church suggests it was once a holy well and perhaps used as a baptistery. Location: on the south side of the churchyard, in the wall along Church Street. SN29222.

Ffynnon Gwyddfaen, Llandyfan – this was clearly an important pilgrimage site. The water was said in 1813 to be 'efficacious in the cure of paralytic affections, numbness and scorbutic humours'. Today the well is a spring-fed pool within solid stone walls, with steps down to a baptism pool. Llandyfan is four miles south of Llandeilo, and the well can be found inside Llandyfan churchyard. SN642171.

Ceredigion

Ffynnon Gybi (St Cybi's Well), Llangybi – an unpretentious spring with the water flowing from under a stone slab in a fenced off corner of a field. Also named 'Ffynnon Wen' as found on the OS map. People seeking a cure for scrofula, rheumatism or scurvy would go to the well on Ascension Eve, wash themselves in the water and then go to a prehistoric stone with the name of Llech Gybi. To be able to sleep under it meant recovery; being unable to sleep meant death. An interesting example of 'incubation' – a practice described in Janet Bord's book *Cures and Curses*. The stone has disappeared, but the well remains. Just off the A485 to the south-west of the village opposite Maesffynnon chapel. Signposted. SN605528.

Ffynnon Llawdog (St Llawdog's Well), Cenarth – a well-presented, well-maintained stone building with a slate roof; and on each end is a slate slab bearing the well's name. It was reputed to be a healing well. It sits on the south bank of the River Teifi in the centre of Cenarth, close to the B4332. SN268416.

Conwy

Ffynnon Gelynin (St Celynin's Well), Llangelynin – to be found in the corner of Llangelynin old church. The water was used for baptisms in the church as well as divination; the clothes of sick children being floated on the water. At the church go up the step-style over the wall on the left, follow the path and over another step-style. Turn left and follow the track to the church. *'Recovery would be indicated if they remained floating, but death was to be the outcome if they sank. After being bathed in the water, the sick children would be carried to a nearby farm where beds were kept in readiness' (JB).* SH751738.

Denbighshire

Ffynnon Beuno (St Beuno's Well), Tremeirchion – the size and depth of the well indicate that this must once have been an important healing well. The well is in the front garden of the house Ffynnon Beuno, formerly an Inn, just south of Tremeirchion on the east side of the B5429 to Bodfari. There is a lay-by in front of the house (now a B&B and restaurant) with an information board to the side. SJ084724.

Ffynnon Degla (St Tegla's Well), Llandegla – this is a healing well. Offerings of pieces of white quartz were once left in the well, many pieces being found during excavation in 1935. Incubation was practised here (cf. Janet Bord, *Cures and Curses*). From the car park near the church in Llandegla (ten miles north of Llangollen) walk down the lane with the church on the right, over the bridge, and the well is signposted across the field to the left. SJ195523.

Ffynnon Fair (St Mary's Well), Cefn Meiriadog – once an important Welsh well shrine, reminiscent of that of St Winefride's Well, both being based on an eight-pointed star. It is hidden deep within the valley of the River Elwy. From Trefnant south of St Asaph, take the B5381. After the hairpin bend and then the crossing of the River Elwy, take the first lane to the left. Continue along the lane and park up the hill by the yellow bin where the lane widens on a bend. Walk back downhill, and take the track to the right past some houses. At the field gate the ruined buildings can be seen across a field to the right; under the trees cross the field (which can be boggy in wet weather). This is private property, but access is tolerated as long as no damage is caused. SJ029711.

Flintshire

Ffynnon Wenfrewy (St Winefride's Well), Treffynnon (Holywell) – the well is still in active use and visited by around 30,000 pilgrims and other visitors each year. Countless cures have been recorded down the centuries and they continue to occur today, with many sick people still coming to follow the traditional bathing ritual (cf. Janet Bord, entry for Holywell, *Cures and Curses*, and on www.saintwinefrideswell. com). In addition to the well building, there can be found a museum, information centre and shop. The well is open daily and details of forthcoming pilgrimages can be found on the website. St Winefride's Well is signposted to Holywell. It is down the hill, beside the B5121 to Greenfield. There is parking opposite the entrance, or in a public car park at the top of the hill nearer the town centre. *'This is without doubt the most impressive holy well in Britain' (JB)*. SJ185763.

Gwynedd

Ffynnon Beuno (St Beuno's Well), Clynnog Fawr – the well is closely linked to nearby St Beuno's Church. His shrine chapel incorporates the site of his first church – eighteen by ten feet – and it was here, after bathing in the well, that sick pilgrims would try to sleep on the saint's tombstone (cf. Janet Bord, 'Incubation' in *Cures and Curses*). The well is not far from the church. A stone-walled structure containing a six-foot square pool is surrounded by stone seats. Clynnog Fawr is nine miles south-west of Caernarfon, and the well is 200 yards down the road from the church, to the south-west and on the opposite side; past the garage, past the last house 'MaesGlas'. SH414495.

Ffynnon Fair (St Mary's Well), Bryncroes – well-maintained structure. May once have been a pilgrimage site. The well is walled around, but not roofed; steps lead down to the water. To be found beside the road, not far from the church at Bryncroes (nine miles north of Pwllheli). SH226314.

Ffynnon Gybi (St Cybi's Well), Llangybi – the well can be found in the valley behind the church in Llangybi village five miles north-east of Pwllheli. Follow the path through the churchyard and across the field down into the valley where the group of ruined stone buildings will be seen below the wood. *'The surviving structures show this to have been a classic healing well, which was once visited by many pilgrims seeking cures for warts, lameness, blindness, scrofula, scurvy and rheumatism' (JB)*. SH427413.

Monmouthshire

St Anne's Well (Virtuous Well), Trellech – a very well-maintained holy well, a short walk from the three dramatic standing stones known as Harold's Stones. The village also has a large Norman castle mound called Tump Terret, and all three historic monuments are depicted on an ancient sundial in the church. The well is an attractive healing well. Found in a field beside a lane to Llandogo, just to the south-east of the village. SO503051.

Pembrokeshire

Bletherston Holy Well – this evocative well, from which water for baptisms used to be fetched, lies below the church. Follow the path down to the pool and the well is tucked away in the corner beside the pool at the end of the path. SN070212.

St Govan's Well, Bosherston – a most dramatically sited well on the shore at the foot of tall cliffs. A beautiful setting: access down a steep flight of stone steps and through the tiny chapel of St Govan, a sixth-century Irish hermit. The well was reputed to be an 'eye' well for the healing of failing eyesight and other diseases. The road from Bosherston to the cliff top is sometimes closed by the Army. If not impeded, there is a large car park from where it is a short walk to the top of the steps. On coming out of the chapel is an attractive small stone well among the rocks. (I once celebrated The Celtic Eucharist with pilgrims at this evocative spot, cf. Brendan O'Malley, *The Celtic Primer*.) SR967929.

Gumfreston Church Wells – Gumfreston is to the west of Tenby, and the wells are in the churchyard. *'Three springs rise close together in the churchyard to the south of the church, two of them being chalybeate and one of them said to be good for the eyes. It was once the custom to throw some crooked pins into the water on Easter Day and in recent years the wells have also been dressed with flowers and plants at Easter'* (JB). SN109010.

Llanllawer Holy Well – a healing 'eye' well. Offerings of pins and coins thrown into the well, the pin bent if harm was intended towards anyone. The well has an attractive stone arched roof, and can be found in a field just outside the churchyard at Llanllawer, two miles south-east of Fishguard, up a steep lane north from Llanychaer Bridge. SM987360.

St Non's Well, St David's – St Non's Chapel marks the site of Saint David's birthplace according to legend, and is dedicated to his mother, St Non. Tradition has it that the place of his birth shone with so serene a light that it glistened as though the sun was visible and God had brought it in front of the clouds. In common with many early Christian churches, the chapel may have been built on a Druidical site. The stones of a Bronze Age stone circle can be seen in the field around it. A further tradition is that to relieve the agony of her labour pains Non supported herself on a stone that lay near her, and that it retained the prints of her fingers. It is said that when the chapel was later built on that spot the stone was introduced as an altar table. Every little chapel had its holy well, many taken over from the Druids and Christianized; the waters used for baptism and the needs of the chapel. St Non's Holy Well was also a healing well, used for rheumatism and eye maladies. The three steps inside and the stone seat for pilgrims are still in place (cf. Brendan O'Malley, 'St David's' in *A Pilgrim's Manual*). It is possible to drive to the well or walk there from St David's; it only being half a mile south of St David's above St Non's Bay. Follow signs for Warpool Court Hotel, then follow the lane past the hotel. SM751243.

Powys

Ffynnon Fair (St Mary's Well), Llanfair Caereinion – when Janet Bord first visited this well it was derelict, but it has now been restored and well worth visiting. It was once a healing well, the large bath showing that it was used for bodily immersion to cure rheumatism and skin diseases. The water was also used for baptisms. The well can be found in the churchyard, downhill between the church and the river. On entering the churchyard walk towards the church but go left around it. SJ104065.

Ffynnon Fair, Pilleth – located close to the church, on the north side of the tower, with steps leading down to it. An 'eye' well. In the Middle Ages pilgrims came to see Our Lady of Pilleth, a wooden statue of Our Lady in the church. The church is on the hillside above Pilleth (four miles north-west of Presteigne) and there is a footpath leading to it. It is possible to drive all the way to the church along a track off the B4356 at SO254679. The well is at SO256683.

St Issui (Isho's/Ishow's)Well, Partrishow/Patrisio/Patricio – a remote 'must visit' well with a shrine chapel and early stone altar which *'may have been the location of the saint's well, and was the place where he was buried' (JB)*. The well is close by, a short way downhill and off to the left on the bend when approached from the church (room to park nearby). It is up against a stone wall and set into the bank. A much decorated well with votive offerings. Partrishow is five miles north-west of Abergavenny, and only accessible along rural lanes. Best approached from Llanfihangel Crucorney: follow the road towards Llanthoney and at Stanton take a left turn, and follow the signs to Partrishow. SO278224.

Ffynnon Myllin, Llanfyllin – this saint could be the Irish St Moling, with both sharing the same feast day, 17 June. Several customs are associated with this well which is set into a steep hillside under a stone arch and a tree, and although a lane leads up to it, it is best not to drive all the way as there is nowhere to turn around. It is only a short walk from the town centre; follow one of the lanes from the central square in a westerly direction. The well is signposted en route. SJ138195.

South Wales

St Cenydd's Well, Llangennith, Gower, Swansea – the well is now a modern spout beneath a stone cover, but once it was roofed with a large stone carved with a cross. It is on the village green not far from the church. SS428914.

Ffynnon Fair (St Mary's Well), Penrhys, Rhondda – an ancient pilgrimage site which was officially restored in 1947. The well is housed in a stone building which is the surviving part of the original well-chapel. It is close to the Penrhys housing estate about four miles north-west of Pontypridd. The route from the car park is a short walk along the main road in a westerly direction, taking the first left down to the footpath sign before turning right on to the grassy track down to the well. *'The area is plagued with vandalism and the well has not escaped, so it has an unloved air about it' (JB)*. ST001945.

SCOTLAND

Aberdeenshire

St Drostan's Well, New Aberdour – the well is on the shore, reached down a winding cliff road, a mile north of New Aberdour, six miles south-west of Fraserburgh. Nearby are the ruins of an old church said to be founded by St Columba; this is also the place where St Drostan landed from Caithness to Christianize the area and found a monastery. NJ887646.

Angus

St Fergus' Well, Glamis – the well is located in woods below the church. It is signposted. NO386469.

Argyle and Bute

St Columba's Well, Keil Point, Southend, Kintyre – the well is close to a ruined chapel and cemetery. The saint's well is twenty yards north-west of the chapel. NR673077.

Holy Well, Kilmory Oib, Tayrallich – the well is found close to a ninth-century cross at the site of the deserted village of Kilmory, Oib. NR780902.

St Ninian's Well (Tobar Ninian), Dervaig, Isle of Mull – behind Kilninian parish church a path between two walls leads to the well. NM357457.

Dumfries and Galloway

Chipperdingan Well, near Port Logan – this name means Tiobar Dingan, or Well of St Ninian. The well is close to the eastern shore of the Rhinns of Galoway at New England Bay.

There is a car park at the entrance to the caravan site. From there walk across the A716 road and the well will be seen across a field. The water flows into a tank. NX120418.

St Queran's Well, Islesteps, Dumfries – a visit to this well is highly recommended by Janet Bord: *'A small circular stone basin with a picture of the saint's face inside contains clear fresh water. When it was cleaned out in 1870 hundreds of coins were found, some dating back to the reign of Elizabeth I. The water was once used for healing, and "clouties" and other offerings are still fastened to the trees.'* She also found that a powerful chalybeate spring was flowing from the stream bank near the bridge only yards away, and wondered whether this was perhaps the true source of the healing water. Located a couple of miles south of Dumfries: a signposted footpath leads from a lane half a mile west of Islesteps to the well. NX956723.

East Lothian

St Baldred's Well, East Lothian – *'St Baldred was a local saint in the eighth century; he spent some time as a hermit on the Bass Rock. After his death, each of his three churches wanted to have his body for burial, and so he caused his remains to be triplicated in order to satisfy them all. His simple well is a stone-lined pool beside the River Tyne, down steps from a path opposite the graveyard of Preston Kirk, one of the churches Baldred founded'* (JB). NT593778.

Rood Well, Stenton – a well-preserved stone well-house standing beside the road to the north-east of the village. NT624744.

Edinburgh

St Anthony's Well, Holyrood Park – the well is a small stone basin beneath a large boulder, on the hillside below St Anthony's Cave and the ruin of the saint's chapel. Located by the footpath leading uphill from St Margaret's Loch towards the chapel. Keep the chapel on the left and look up the slope for the large boulder. The water was once believed to have healing properties, and it was also customary on May Day to bathe one's face in the dew on Arthur's Seat; then make a wish at the well. NT275736.

St Mungo's Well, Currie – on the Water of Leith Walkway close to Currie Kirk, this small well with a stone surround may date from the time of the earliest church on this site. NT184677.

Fife

St Fillan's Well, Pittenweem – access is in Cove Wynd. *'St Fillan, an eighth-century abbot, lived at Pittenweem (which means "town of the cave"); supposedly in St Fillan's Cave by the harbour. His well, a small pool, can still be found in the cave (on the far left side). It was rededicated for worship in 1935' (JB).* NO550024.

Highland

St Boniface's Well (Cloutie Well) – a well festooned with clouties (rags). A former wishing well, now a healing well, it consists of a pipe in the bank from which the water flows into a small stone basin. Located beside a lay-by on the south side of the A832 north-west of Munlochy. NH641537.

St Ignatius' Well, Glassburn – the stone well-house, which was reconstructed in 1880, is topped by a large cross and bears a plate with many names, dates and inscriptions. NH370344.

St John the Baptist's Well, Fodderty – a healing well, especially for mental issues, with clouties on the bushes. Located up a hill south of Fodderty: from Dingwall turn left before Fodderty Church on a lane passing Fodderty Lodge, park at the end and follow footpath from there. NH514588.

St Mary's Well, Culloden – still much frequented, with coins thrown into the water as offerings, and clouties. The well is surrounded by an unroofed stone wall. Located in Forestry Commission woodland. Access via Blackpark Farm from the B9006, south-east of Inverness. NH723453.

St Ninian's Well, Drumnadrochit – a healing well with rags (clouties) left by pilgrims. Close to the church, this well is near the standing stone marking the site of a Knights Templar house by Temple Pier. NH530300.

Isle of Skye

Tobar Ashik (St Maelrubha's Well), Broadford – Maelrubha was an eighth-century monk who founded a monastery at Applecross, from where he evangelized Skye. A chapel may have stood close to this well, and a cross-engraved stone has been found. The well is easily reached from a lane north of the A850, two miles north-east of Broadford. NG687242.

Moray

St Furnac's Well, Botriphnie – the well is on the east of the churchyard, which has the ruins of an earlier chapel where a wooden image of the saint was once kept. The well is a circular stone-lined hole in the ground on the route of a wildlife walk in the area of Drummuir Castle and Loch Park. NJ376443.

Perth and Kinross

St David's Well, Weem – two springs flow into stone basins from a rock outcrop on a hill behind Weem Church; reached by a footpath starting alongside the church. The name was originally St Cuthbert's Well because of his connection with it. Weem is nine miles south-west of Pitlochry. NN843501.